PALM

Reaktion's Botanical series is the first of its kind, integrating horticultural and botanical writing with a broader account of the cultural and social impact of trees, plants and flowers.

PALM

Fred Gray

REAKTION BOOKS

For Carol, with my thanks for the enduring encounter

Published by
REAKTION BOOKS LTD
Unit 32, Waterside
44–48 Wharf Road
London N1 7UX, UK

www.reaktionbooks.co.uk

First published 2018

Printed and bound in China

A catalogue record for this book is available from the British Library

ISBN 978 1 78023 917 0

Contents

✣

The celebrated coco de mer palm, endemic to just two
of the 115 islands in the Seychelles archipelago.

one

The Prince of Plants

✤

Contemporary cities are full of palms, past and present, real and imagined. Take one city, London, and a journey guided by the River Thames as it flows from west to east, heading towards the sea.

The starting point is Kew in West London, and the home of the Royal Botanic Gardens with its internationally famed plant collection. Here are London's most spectacular living palms, in a state of vigorous health. Visually stunning coconut, peach, queen and babassu palms soar upwards towards the roof of the central dome of the Palm House, constructed between 1844 and 1848. The structure, a bold statement of the Victorian quest to understand and capture exotic palms and display them for the edification of the capital's inhabitants, is one of the world's most important surviving nineteenth-century iron and glass buildings.

To the east and close to the Houses of Parliament is Tate Britain, the home of the foremost collection of British art in the world. The 1960s gallery features David Hockney's iconic painting *A Bigger Splash* (1967); its combination of palm trees, swimming pool, modernist architecture and sunshine helping to express the artist's California dreaming.

A mile to the north, the most famous gates in Britain for over a century guard the entrance to Buckingham Palace, the official London residence of the reigning monarch of the United Kingdom. Hung in 1911, the gates feature the royal coat of arms encircled by golden palm leaves. Across from the gates stands the dominating Victoria Memorial, erected to commemorate the death of Queen Victoria in 1901. In a palpable symbol of British might and global power, at the apex of the memorial a gilded bronze figure, Winged Victory, stands on a globe with a victor's palm held in one hand.

Across Green Park from the royal palace is eighteenth-century Spencer House, the capital's finest surviving aristocratic palace. The building's extraordinary Palm Room, a product of ideas about classical architecture and nature, is a theatrical stage set; gilded columns become make-believe palm stems and from these flow abstracted palm fronds.

One of the capital's Victorian grand railway hotels, now known as the Landmark London, is a further forty-minute walk along the streets of London. When it opened in 1899 the public rooms of what was then the Great Central Hotel were embellished with potted palms. Today the hotel's Winter Garden restaurant boasts a preposterous array of seemingly real palms; despite their appearance, these are 'preserved' palms – once living plants that have been dismembered, embalmed, reconstructed and transformed into decorative objects.

Form follows function: exterior of the Palm House, Royal Botanic Garden, Kew. The captive palms rear up within the building.

Palms of pleasure and dreaming. David Hockney, *A Bigger Splash*, 1967, acrylic paint on canvas.

Downstream further still, St Paul's Cathedral stands serenely on rising ground close to the river. The great religious building hosts varied palm motifs. Palm fronds have long been used as a symbol of victory and, in Christianity, as a sign of triumph over death. In the crypt, the mosaic floor surrounding the tomb of Lord Nelson (1758–1821), the nation's supreme naval hero, contains images of palm trees and the admiral's motto, *Palmam qui meruit ferat* – 'Let he who has earned it bear the palm'. High on the cathedral's quire ceiling another mosaic depicts the creation of animals, with lions, tigers, elephants, camels and other creatures gamboling amid palm trees.

A short stroll from St Paul's leads to St Botolph without Aldersgate, a medieval church rebuilt in the late eighteenth century and with a pulpit standing fancifully on a wooden palm stem. A mile to the west, the Museum of London contains images of palm fronds and branches that have survived in the city for almost two millennia: these are on coins once used as currency in Roman Londinium and subsequently recovered from the archaeological sediments. Nearby, the capital's great storehouse of world art and artefacts, the British Museum, has an astoundingly diverse and outstanding array of palm images and objects collected over 250 years and reverberating with Britain's imperial past. Searching the museum's collection online reveals twenty thousand 'palm' results, 2,500 for coconut, 2,000 for rattan, 1,100 for coir, 950 for date palm and 457 for sago.

Both museums border the City of London, one of the world's financial capitals. Beginning with trade and auctions in eighteenth-century coffee houses, for more than two centuries this city has been one of the international centres for buying and selling palm raw materials and products. On the north bank of the river by Blackfriars Bridge is the building housing the British headquarters of Unilever,

Buckingham Palace sightseers in October 2016 dwarfed by one set of the massive iron gates, embellished by the royal crest enclosed by palm fronds.

The gilded 'Winged Victory', symbolic palm branch held in her left hand, provides the pinnacle of the early 20th-century Victoria Memorial. The Mall, London. The memorial is a rich allegorical statement about the power and magnificence of the British empire.

one of the world's largest companies using palm oil derivatives in the manufacture of foodstuffs and consumer goods including personal and home care products. The early 1930s lamp standards guarding the building's main entrance are adorned with imagined images of Africans engaged in heroic feats or working with palms in their native habitat.

The Thames was a great commercial artery accommodating shipping wharfs and a complex dock system where, for over two centuries, palms and palm products were imported from the tropical world in ever-greater profusion. Close to the river were factories making soap, candles, margarine and biscuits from palm oils and fats. Just south

'Preserved palms' adorn the Winter Garden restaurant of the Landmark, London –
once a grand railway hotel decorated with potted palms.

of Tower Bridge, Bermondsey, where the smell of biscuit-making pervaded the air, was also known as 'Biscuit Town'. The largest candle factory in the world was on the riverside at Battersea, built on the site of a former coconut-crushing works that extracted hard fats for candles. A century ago the Maypole Margarine Factory in Southall, West London, was the largest in Europe.

The majority of these palm-using factories are long closed. The final point on this London palm itinerary, however, is the Unilever food spreads factory at Purfleet, close to the Thames and 32 km (20 miles) east of the company's headquarters in the City of London. With palm oil a critical ingredient, the Purfleet plant has produced margarine and similar products for more than a century. Today it is reputedly the world's largest factory for the manufacture of food spreads, producing one million tubs – of various sizes – a day.

Modern food spreads are one instance – there are legions of others – of how the palm has inveigled and seduced itself into the daily lives of London's inhabitants and visitors. Whether as a photograph in a magazine, an image on television or an ingredient in fast-moving consumer goods bought from a supermarket or convenience store, nowadays it is impossible, bar the most exceptional circumstances, for people to avoid daily contact with palms. Modern London, in this sense, is like all modern cities: a city of the palm.

As the capital city of a former world power, with an empire on which the sun never set, London has a particularly rich palmography. Similar journeys in search of the palm might also be undertaken in cities and towns around the world. Palm itineraries suggest and expose varied themes – themes that this book explores – about how and why the plant has come to assume such significance for contemporary places and contemporary people.

Themes and Boundaries

Palms are extraordinary flowering plants. The quintessential tropical tree, everyone knows how the archetypal palm looks and most people can have a good stab at drawing one from memory. The eighteenth-century Swedish botanist Carl Linnaeus (1707–1778), who was responsible for formalizing the scientific naming system for species of living things, which is still in use today, believed the palm was the 'prince of plants' because of its 'noble and impressive shape'.[1] Despite the recognizable and distinctive stereotypes, this botanical family is also amazingly diverse. There are over 2,600 and perhaps as many as 3,000 individual palm species, with the figure continually rising as new palms are discovered and classification systems improve.

Palms are the consummate record-breakers in the vegetative world. The coco de mer palm, *Lodoicea maldivica*, produces the world's biggest and heaviest seed, weighing up to 30 kg (66 lb); because of the resemblance to an abstracted female form, the seed is sometimes known as the love nut. The plant kingdom's longest leaf, 25 m (82 ft) or more long and 3 m (10 ft) wide, grows on the African raffia palm, *Raphia regalis*. At 10 m (33 ft) tall and with up to 24 million tiny flowers, the earth's largest inflorescence – a group or cluster of flowers carried on a stem – grows on *Corypha umbraculifera*, the talipot palm of India. The record for the longest stem of any plant, at nearly 200 m (655 ft), is held by *Calamus manan*, a species of climbing rattan, which scale existing trees but sometimes spread horizontally across the forest floor. Visually more impressive and more obviously tree-like, Colombia's national tree, the wax palm, *Ceroxylon quindiuense*, has an unbranched aerial stem that soars up to 60 m (197 ft) before being topped by its crown.

Despite the common use of the phrase 'palm tree', the plant is not a tree comparable to deciduous broadleaves or evergreen conifers. It does not have a woody trunk that thickens each year by growing outwards; it does not produce annual growth rings and is not covered by an outer layer of bark. Instead, palms have more in common with

Coco de mer fruit, Praslin Island, Seychelles, 1851–1930.

herbs and grasses. The botanic distinctiveness of the palm and its natural history is explored in the next chapter. The focus is on both the development of scientific understanding of palms during the nineteenth century – the key period of discovery and exploitation – and how modern biology and botany has classified and dissected the plant. The vast majority of palm species are native to the world's tropical and subtropical zones. In these homelands the palm plays a critical role, sketched out in the conclusion of the chapter, in sustaining indigenous peoples, including those living in remote and isolated rainforest communities, and in the development of more advanced historic societies, such as those in Southeast Asia.

Chapter Three turns to the role of one species of palm, the date palm, *Phoenix dactylifera*, in the birth and development millennia ago of the ancient civilizations in the Middle East's Fertile Crescent, the irregular semicircle of land reaching from the Nile valley in the west to the Persian Gulf in the east. The date palm did not just have practical and functional utility; people nurtured and cultivated their relationships with the plant, and it acquired mystical, sacred and

A Coconut charm, Papuan Gulf area, New Guinea, made from a dwarf coconut and representing a swordfish, c. 1890–1920. The charm would have been filled with magical substances. The fibre bag allowed travellers to carry the charm around their necks to ward off danger.

Lithograph of a painting by David Roberts, *Temple at Esneh*, dated 25 November 1838.

symbolic meanings that have reverberated across millennia to the present day.

The story of how the palm was discovered by the West is told in Chapter Four. From uncertain beginnings, the process took hundreds of years, although the pace of discovery and understanding sped up with the emergence of the modern world, voyages of Western exploration from Europe to tropical lands, embryonic international trade and the birth of the Industrial Revolution.

Capitalism, as it developed and spread around the world, understood and exploited the palm in new and extraordinary ways. In Chapter Five the narrative moves on to look at how, in the era of industry and empire, the palm became one of the major natural resources exploited in the West's tropical and subtropical empires. Palms and palm products were transported back, to the heart of the empire, to lubricate (sometimes literally so) the engines of capitalism. Oils and fats from palms became a key ingredient in the making of soap, one of the first modern consumer products.

More than any other plant, the palm is today deeply and intricately embedded in modern consumer societies as both reality and idea. Some of our contemporary relationships with palms and palm products are obscure or concealed; some are controversial and unwelcome; others are joyous and celebratory.

Chapter Six describes the economic exploitation of palm oils during the post-war period to the present day. Contemporary use of palm oils is often hidden from view but is mired in controversy. Used as an ingredient in everything from instant noodles to cookies and from shampoo to lipstick, palm oils have helped to define what it means to be a consumer in the modern world. But what are perhaps the world's most important and omnipresent modern ingredients derived from a plant are also implicated in the destruction of tropical rainforest, its flora and fauna, and traditional communities.

The dramatic palm: the frontispiece of Sophy Moody's *The Palm Tree* (1864).

The architectural palm: Al Zumerida, Kuwait, April 2011.

The final three chapters shift to other themes and ideas. Captured and transported, from the nineteenth century the palm was taken to new places beyond its natural homelands and used, as an ornamental and architectural plant, as clothing and to romanticize and glamorize exterior places as diverse as coastal gardens in western Britain, the promenades of the French Riviera and Hollywood boulevards. Where the palm could not survive outside, it was caged in artificial environments, including palm houses and winter gardens, and exhibited for the wonderment of people living in colder northern climes.

The final chapter turns to the palm of abstractions and fantasies. Reduced to its idealized essential elements and made artificial, the palm motif in decoration and design has long been an important

Palms in El Parque de Malaga: a harbour-side public garden, Malaga, Spain, 2009.

signifier, although precisely what is indicated has evolved over time. As a fantasy, the palm has become a convenient shorthand to suggest a complex of interrelated, although at times contradictory, ideas and emotions. Today it is often a symbol of non-work and being at leisure, of pleasurable other worlds and dream worlds, of the exotic, the erotic, the remote and isolated, and being away from civilization and close to nature. At times the reverse is the case and the palm may imply danger and the destruction of civilization.

two
Dissecting the Giant Herb
꙾

I n the sixteenth century the words 'tropics' and 'tropical' emerged as catch-alls used by Europeans to describe the lands and seas girdling the equator. Travellers and explorers from Europe wanted to understand – and subsequently exploit and dominate – the varied peoples and geographies of the lands they had discovered. The palm was soon recognized as the quintessential tropical and subtropical plant. First natural philosophers and natural historians and then, from the seventeenth century, botanists set about studying, dissecting, cataloguing and classifying the plant.

Europeans were particularly impressed by the look, shape and uniqueness of the palm. Prussian explorer and naturalist Alexander von Humboldt (1769–1859) thought palms 'the stateliest of all vegetable forms'.[1] In 1786 the extraordinary German literary figure Johann Wolfgang von Goethe (1749–1832) visited the botanical gardens in Padua (the first to be established in Europe in 1545). He thought the two-hundred-year-old specimen of the European fan palm, *Chamaerops humilis*, he saw there might lead him closer to the idea of the *Urpflanze*, the archetypal or ancestral plant.

Their magnificence apart, it became clear that palms were very different from typical European trees and other woody plants. Palm 'trees', despite the common usage of the term, do not have trunks, wood or bark and, unlike trees proper, cannot increase in diameter through secondary growth. Palms are essentially giant herbs. Along with plants such as orchids, grasses and grains, bananas, onions,

Tab .91.

MAXIMILIANA regia.

Illustrations of palms in their natural habitats were a critical means of classifying and disseminating information about different species. This 1826 illustration of the botanical illustrator at work is by the influential German botanist and explorer Carl Friedrich Philipp von Martius and was published in his *Historia naturalis palmarum 1.*

asparagus and flowering bulbs from bluebells to tulips, palms are monocots, one of the three classes of flowering plants. The seeds of monocots contain just one cotyledon, the embryonic or seed leaf that uses a seed's nutrients to produce the first true leaves, which grow in turn from a single point.

The Puzzle of Classification

The naming and classification of palms has been a work in progress for over two centuries. The taxonomists – those responsible for producing systems of classification – have argued and debated over what the ordering should be and which botanical characteristics to prioritize. During the great age of Western plant exploration the same species was sometimes 'discovered' by different botanists, each inventing or allocating a different scientific name. Confusion and turf wars often reigned.

Take the wonderfully ornamental and architectural red latan palm from Réunion, the remote island in the Western Indian Ocean. European natural philosophers identified it as a separate species in the last decade of the eighteenth century. The German physician and botanist Joseph Gaertner was first, naming it *Cleophora lontaroides* in 1791. A year later another German, Johann Friedrich Gmelin, called it *Latania commersonii*, while a French naturalist and soldier, Jean-Baptiste Lamarck, used the name *Latania borbonica*. For the Dutchman Baron Nikolaus von Jacquin in 1800, it was *Latania rubra*. Although the species name was argued over, the genus name, *Latania* – a Latinization of the local common name *latinier* – seemed established. But some disagreed. Seven decades later the London nurseryman and horticultural writer Benjamin Samuel Williams thought it belonged to a different genus and named it *Livistona borbonica* in his book *Choice Stove and Greenhouse Ornamental-leaved Plants* (1870). *Latania plagicoma* followed in 1877 and *Latania vera* in 1895. In 1941 the American botanist Orator Fuller Cook, returning to the original genus name, thought the palm should be called *Cleophora commersonii*. Finally, in 1963, the great palm botanist and classifier Harold Emery Moore (1917–1980) awarded what was to become the recognized and accepted scientific name, *Latania lontaroides*.[2]

Another level of complexity concerned how to classify and structure the overarching palm order: what elements or characteristics of palms were critical in distinguishing one species from another or uniting different species as members of the same family or subfamily. Carl Friedrich Philipp von Martius (1794–1868) made the first noteworthy attempt to provide a classificatory framework. An explorer, botanist and academic, Martius travelled in the Amazon basin for three years from 1817. On returning to Germany, his remarkable, monumental and beautifully illustrated *Historia naturalis palmarum* (Natural History of Palms) was published in three volumes between 1823 and

1850. Basing his framework on his study of the reproductive elements of palms, Martius thought there were six different palm families.

At much the same time, other botanists, with field experience in other parts of the world, put forward alternative frameworks and nomenclatures. William Griffith (1810–1845), working in India in the 1840s, was the first plant scientist to explicitly adopt the approach that continues today, treating palms as a single botanical family containing a number of subfamilies.

From the middle of the nineteenth century palm explorers and botanists, while advancing scientific knowledge of palms, also wrote about the plant for an expanding and avid general readership. Two of the most notable writers of popular palm books were Alfred Russel Wallace (1823–1913), the author of *Palm Trees of the Amazon and Their*

Botanical illustrations were often copied – as in this alternative 1855 version of the Martius original, redrawn by L. Stroobant for *L'Illustration horticole*. The new artist changed the social relations of the palm illustrator.

Uses, and Berthold Seemann (1825–1871), the writer of *Popular History of the Palms and Their Allies*. Both the young scientists — they were in their early thirties when their books were published in the 1850s — had already each spent four years as naturalists exploring the world. Both men were brilliant polymaths, although Seemann died in his forties while Wallace, by the time of his death in 1913, was probably the world's most famous scientist.

Wallace's opening paragraph still has a freshness and relevance in the twenty-first century:

> Palms are endogenous or ingrowing plants, belonging to the same great division of the Vegetable Kingdom as the Grasses, Bamboos, Lilies and Pineapples, and not to which contains all our English forest trees. They are perennial, not annual . . . Their stems are simple or very rarely forked, slender, erect, and cylindrical, not tapering as in most other trees; they are hardest on the outside, and are marked more or less distinctly with scars or rings, marking the situation of the fallen leaves.[3]

Noting that fewer than six hundred palm species were then known, with remarkable foresight Wallace proposed that 2,000 species was a more probable estimate.

Older classification systems were amended and new ones proposed throughout the twentieth century, typically on the basis of prioritizing different aspects of palm morphology   the form and structure of the plant — such as the formation and form of the leaf, the character of the stem and the method of germination. The grouping into subfamilies, although based on descriptive palm morphology, also supposed that all the species in each subfamily were related to each other.[4]

The transformative classificatory development, since the 1990s, has been the revolution in understanding the evolutionary relationships between palm species. The advance, one result of wider radical

Preparing a young coconut to access the clear water in the fruit's centre.
Roadside coconut seller, Saint Lucia, 2016.

advances in plant phylogenetics, uses DNA sequencing to understand the molecular structure and evolution of palms. A more rigorous and more certain classification is the result, and is presented in detail in the imperious *Genera Palmarum* (2008). At last proven science, rather than speculation backed by mere description, is able to demonstrate that all the palms within a subfamily are descended from a common ancestor.[5]

However, as it has been for over two centuries, the classification of palms remains a work in progress. Despite the recent advances, the current framework will be amended and developed further and the number of palm genera and species will be revised upwards as new molecular and morphological studies are undertaken, botanical knowledge is finessed and additional palm species are discovered.

In contemporary botanical classification, palms are in an overarching monocot order, Arecales. This itself contains a single plant family, Arecaceae, which, for historical reasons, and confusingly, is alternatively known as Palmae. Arecaceae has five subfamilies – Calamoideae, Nypoideae, Coryphoideae, Ceroxyloideae and finally Arecoideae – and, in turn, 28 tribes and 27 subtribes. Finally, and depending on the sources used, there are between 180 and 200 palm genera and between 2,600 and 3,000 individual species.

For example, that most emblematic tropical plant and the one truly pan-tropical palm species, the coconut palm, which has the species name *Cocos nucifera*, is of the genus *Cocos*, the tribe Cocoseae, the subfamily Arecoideae, and so to the all-embracing family and order names, Arecaceae and Arecales.

Extremes of Diversity

Palms have existed for millions of years. The oldest palm fossils date from the Cretaceous period, 100 million years ago. Today, and as the large number of species suggests, palms display an astounding diversity of form. While the quintessential palm has a solitary and erect

The spectacular diamond-shaped leaves of the stemless Joey palm, *Johannesteijsmannia altifrons*, on display in Cairns Botanic Gardens, Queensland, Australia.

Using long and hooked tendrils the lawyer cane, *Calamus australis*, claws and lassoes itself to the rainforest canopy in northeast Queensland, Australia.

aerial stem topped by a crown of large evergreen leaves, there are other possibilities, including regular branching in just a few species.

Some grow horizontally, along or just under the ground, and produce a crown at ground level. Palms are especially at home in the soft mud of tropical tidal estuaries, creeks and rivers. For example, the mangrove palm, *Nypa fruticans* (the only species in the palm subfamily Nypoideae), which is distributed across the vast area from the Ganges Delta to the array of large and small islands in the Southwest Pacific, has stems that grow horizontally just beneath the surface, from which large leaf fronds emerge and soar upwards.

Other palms are vines that attach themselves to established trees and climb up to forest canopies. Some climbing rattans, from the genus *Calamus*, have extraordinary life stories: clawing and hooking their way into the forest canopy and then, if the weight-support mechanisms fail, the plants may fall back to sprawl, still growing, on the forest floor before attempting to ascend yet again. The stems of one rattan species, *Calamus manan*, recorded at almost 200 m (655 ft), are longer than those of any other plant.

The palms holding records for great size, height and length are balanced by the small and slight. The palm family contains species that are just 12 cm (4.7 in.) high and others that are 60 m (195 ft) tall; stem diameters vary from a mere 3 mm to well over 1 m (3 ft).

The diameter of a palm stem is determined underground before the plant grows upwards. Growth occurs at the extremities of the plant, both in the roots and in the topping crown of leaves. As the plant grows the stem becomes enclosed by an exterior sheath made up of the remains of overlapping leaf bases. As new leaves grow, from a single point at the apex of the stem, so the older leaves are effectively pushed down the stem. A stem's centre is usually spongy, softer and with a greater volume than the areas towards the periphery. These tend to be made of bundles of hard and dense cells, fibres and

The dangerous job
of tapping the sap
of a palm tree from
which palm wine
is made, Nigeria,
c. 1970.

connecting strands, which, strengthening and thickening over time, are capable of blunting tools used in attempts to slice through them. Palm stems have been compared with steel-reinforced concrete columns: hard, strong and yet with flexibility, the capacity to bend and great resistance to breakage.[6]

Roots typically plunge into the ground, but some form a mound above ground level or emerge higher up a stem, acting as props or stilts. The evergreen leaves have varied forms but all are plicate – with accordion-like folds – and the two classic leaf shapes are pinnate or palmate, resembling, respectively, a feather and a fan. Palm flowers are carried on an extraordinary range of inflorescences, including massive complicated clusters of hundreds of flowers. The most wondrous example of an inflorescence with many millions of minute flowers is the talipot palm, *Corypha umbraculifera*, which flowers and fruits once in its lifetime of between thirty and eighty years and then dies. There is also significant variation in other aspects of palm architecture and morphology, including the size, shape and development of the stem, roots and leaves; the branching pattern; and the reproductive apparatus of the plant, including the structure of the flower and its component parts.

Palm fruit are usually single-seeded drupes or stone fruit: typically the pericarp surrounding the seed is made up of an outer skin, or exocarp, which itself contains a fleshy mesocarp within which sits the hard endocarp, or stone protecting and holding the seed or kernel. Two palm fruits with immense human utility, those of the date palm, *Phoenix dactylifera*, and oil palm, *Elaeis guineensis*, have fleshy mesocarps; in contrast, the mesocarp of the similarly useful coconut develops into a fibrous dry husk.

Palm Geographies

The homelands of more than 90 per cent of palm species are the hot and humid, moist or wet tropical rainforests. Because of their geographical origins, palms do not require a protective dormancy

Looking over tropical rainforest towards Petit Piton, Saint Lucia, 2016.
Palms frame 'the view' of many iconic tropical landscapes.

mechanism allowing them to shut down in order to survive periods of intense and prolonged cold; and the absence of this mechanism limits the ability of palms to survive beyond their native lands.

With 992 species, by far the most palm-rich biogeographical region is Malesia. Straddling the equator and located in the Southwest Pacific Ocean between mainland Southeast Asia and Australia, the region embraces the Malay Peninsula and hundreds of islands, including the Philippines, Sumatra and Borneo. Other parts of the Pacific, including the archetypal palm islands of Fiji and Hawaii, have 128 species and Australasia has 58. The Americas host 730 native palm species: 437 are in South America, 251 in Central America, 238 are on the islands of the Caribbean and only fourteen are in North America. Given that the equator bisects the continent, Africa has a surprising paucity of palms, with just 65 species. To the east of Africa, islands in the Western Indian Ocean provide the homelands for 193 species; with 165 endemic palm species, Madagascar, the world's

fourth-largest island, has almost three times as many species as the whole of continental Africa. In the vast area of mainland Asia there are 354 indigenous palm species. Despite the role of Europeans in dissecting and classifying the palm family, Europe has exactly two species, one of them shared with Africa and the other with Asia.[7]

In stark contrast to the palm's iconic association with the tropics, it is also sometimes presented as a symbol of desert landscapes, including desert oases and islands. However, the palm's roots need an abundance of water for the plant to survive and prosper. In the desert Coachella Valley in southern California, for example, oases of the California fan palm, *Washingtonia filifera*, follow the spring line created by the San Andreas earthquake fault.

Palms tolerant of high elevations or latitude extremes are able to prosper away from classical lowland rainforest. A species of dramatically tall Andean wax palm, *Ceroxylon parvifrons*, holds the elevation record, growing in Ecuador's high cloud forest sometimes at almost 3,600 m (2.2 miles) above sea level. Far from the tropics, the northernmost indigenous palm, *Chamaerops humilis*, the European fan palm, grows at 44°N in coastal Mediterranean France. At much the same latitude in the southern hemisphere the world's most southerly palm, *Rhopalostylis sapida*, a species of nīkau palm, grows on the remote Chatham Islands in the Pacific Ocean to the east of New Zealand.

A particularly cold-tolerant species is *Trachycarpus fortunei*, variously known as the Chusan palm, Chinese windmill palm, windmill palm and just the fan palm. First brought to Europe from Japan in 1830 and then from China in 1849, the palm is now naturalized in the Italian Lakes and southern Switzerland, further to the north and at higher elevations than the native European fan palm. Exotic palms in wintery Alpine landscapes make for wonderfully incongruous images. Used as exotic architectural plants, Chusans also adorn temperate and

opposite: A grove of the ornamental lipstick or red sealing wax palm, *Cyrtostachys renda*, in Cairns Botanic Gardens, Queensland, Australia.

overleaf: Washingtonia filifera in the southern California Desert.

Chusan palms at home on the Italian Lakes: the view from the gardens of the Villa del Balbianello, Lenno, Lake Como, 2014.

especially coastal landscapes at much higher latitudes in Europe and North America.

In benign environments particular palms may grow in abundance, forming dense, massive stands and colonies covering large areas: single species of palms dominate in many tropical estuaries, marshes and swamplands. In much of the Amazon basin, with an estimated 400 billion woody trees and palms belonging to 16,000 different species, the situation is different.[8] However, despite the huge region's botanical richness and diversity, there are relatively few 'hyperdominant' Amazonian trees or palms; of the twenty most dominant, seven are palms. The most common plant of all, with 5.2 billion specimens, is the Assai palm, *Euterpe precatoria*. In fifth place, with an estimated 4 billion plants, is *Iriartea deltoidea*, a palm with many common and vernacular names, including the stilt, horn or barrigona (pot-bellied) palm.

Palms and Indigenous Societies

Distinguished by its dense and tough outer stem with, unusually, a swollen central section, *Iriartea deltoidea* – like all the species mentioned in this chapter – has been utilized by humans in varied ways. With the stem spilt open and the softer inner sections of the stem removed, the remaining hard, durable outer parts have been used for walls, flooring, making spears and, in the case of the bulging stem, even as canoes and coffins.[9]

In its homelands the palm has, for millennia, sustained people and nurtured communities. The plant's resources have helped civilizations to bloom, economies to prosper and cultures to flourish. Societies have, in turn, endowed the palm with symbolic and sacred meanings. Reflecting immense ingenuity in people's dealings with the vegetative world, the diversity of palm uses has been astounding, with the plant employed to make everything from medicines to weapons, from clothing to sails for ocean-going ships and from alcoholic beverages to lotions for the hair and body.[10]

A classic early 1980s ethnobotanical study examined the use of seventeen palm species by the Apinayé and Guajajara tribes of northeast Brazil.[11] The most important, the babassu palm (identified as *Orbignya phalerata* and now classified as a species of the genus *Attalea*) had a vast range of uses: the liquid endosperm in the kernels, for instance, was used to stem bleeding; the husks provided an anaesthetic to reduce toothache and, when burnt, the smoke repelled insects; the mesocarp was used as a bait when hunting rodents; the leaves were burnt to provide agricultural nutrients; and the stems were a valuable construction material. Such uses declined as the two tribes were increasingly exposed to outside influences.

Practical utility aside, for the tribes of the Amazon basin palms have also had spiritual, magical and supernatural dimensions, often associated with tribal origin stories. To take one example, the Makuna people of the Pira Paraná River in the Colombian Amazon believe that the spirits of their female ancestors are reincarnated in a specific palm (*Jessenia bataua*; now named *Oenocarpus bataua*) and, through the palm fruit, continue to feed the living with their breast milk.[12] Multiply and diversify such beliefs throughout the tropical and subtropical world and, although much knowledge is now lost, it is apparent that

An opaque watercolour on a palm leaf, early 12th century, Bengal or Bangladesh. Image of seated White Tara in a flame-emitting aureole.

for many indigenous peoples the palm has had deep mystical and religious significance.

In other palm homelands, such as Southeast Asia, far more industrialized societies had long exploited the palm in intricate and complex ways. Writing in the middle of the nineteenth century Edward Balfour, the Deputy Inspector General of the Madras Army, described a Tamil poem, 'The Tala Vilásam', which enumerated 801 uses of the palmyra palm, *Borassus flabellifer*.[13] For over two millennia one of the uses of this palm was for the leaves to be dried and smoked and then used as manuscripts to be written on and to carry illustrations; writing, in turn, allowed information and ideas to pass between people and across generations, and enabled societies to develop further. By the time Balfour's book was printed and distributed the use of palm-leaf manuscripts was in decline; those that remain are nowadays preserved carefully and valued both as artefacts and for the information they contain.

three

The Civilizing Date

꙰

One palm, the date palm, *Phoenix dactylifera*, is bound up with the development of settled agriculture in the Old World and the emergence of cities and civilizations; from these roots and over millennia has emerged today's Western civilization. Without the date palm the modern world, as it is now, would not exist.

The date palm was probably the first of the quartet of fruit trees to be originally domesticated in the Old World. Unlike the other three – the olive, grapevine and fig found wild in the lands rimming the Mediterranean – the date palm was domesticated in the ancient Near East (also known as the Middle East and, less Eurocentrically, Western Asia). The earliest archaeological date remains that are associated with humans, from eight millennia ago, are probably of wild dates. Although it is uncertain precisely when and where the date was domesticated, it was most likely during the Chalcolithic period, the first step into the Bronze Age from the Neolithic, between 6,500 and 5,500 years ago, and the place may have been a desert oasis or the lower Mesopotamian basin – the area stretching from Baghdad to the Persian Gulf.[1]

Arab folklore summarizes the date palm's preferred ecology with the saying, 'The king of the oasis bathes his feet in water and his head is in heaven's fire.'[2] Although the plant is able to survive periods of drought and salty, stagnant water, it flourishes where its roots have ready access to sweet water, and in such conditions the palm prospered

The products of millennia of cultivation, date groves remain a dominant landscape feature on the banks of the Tigris River. Photograph, *c.* 1932, taken over Iraq (ancient Babylonia).

'Iraq. River scenes on the Euphrates taken at Hilla. Drying fishing nets. Hung from stately palms.' Photograph taken in 1932.

in the warm deserts of Arabia and the Sahara. An immensely impressive and productive plant, a single date palm may grow to a height of 24 m (79 ft) and have a crown spanning more than 9 m (30 ft). There were (and still are) hundreds of varieties of date palm cultivars, each producing dates with different characteristics; the most productive plants, which may live for more than a century, yield dozens of pounds of fruit each year. Multiply a single plant into a date palm orchard and the visual result is a striking botanical regiment on parade.

Tamed and Employed

Domestication transformed the reproductive biology of the plant from untrammelled sexual reproduction in the wild (through wind pollination) to the tamed and controlled vegetative propagation of the plant in captivity. A dioecious species – the male and female reproductive organs are in separate plants – hand-pollination carried out by skilled workers first occurred more than 4,000 years ago. In a botanical version of the harem, just one male plant was required to pollinate fifty or more date-producing female plants.

The plant itself was reproduced through two means: either planting the seed or transplanting offshoots. The first method made it straightforward to spread the date palm from one place to another, since the seed or pit within the fruit could survive for a long period and was uncomplicated to germinate. (In 2005 a 2,000-year-old male date seed recovered during excavations of the ruined fortress of Masada was germinated successfully and a decade later was used to pollinate a female plant.)[3] However, planting from seed led to variable adult date palms and too many male plants, so instead the preferred reproductive strategy was to transplant rooted offshoots from exceptional individual plants that delivered the required traits.[4]

The domestication and cultivation of the date palm required a settled society. Custom, practice and law were employed to guard and regulate the use of the plant. For example, the Babylonian Code of Hammurabi, from about 1750 BCE (and one of the world's oldest

Irrigated palm groves helped sustain a diverse microagricultural system, including cornfields. Photograph of the Nile valley, Egypt, taken between 1934 and 1939.

deciphered writings of a substantial length) details the law and sanctions applicable to the planting and farming of date orchards and relationships between landowners and palm gardeners.[5] At the same time there was also an increasingly elaborate technical apparatus available, including complex irrigation systems and machinery such as date presses to extract syrup from the fruit. Date farmers also developed skilled specialisms, such as hand pollination and tending, detaching and transplanting offshoots.

Communities needed to be secure from destructive marauding invaders; where such conditions were absent the results could be catastrophic. Some surviving Assyrian monuments, for instance, portray the destruction of the date orchards belonging to besieged or captured cities, although such acts of economic warfare were more than matched by a victor's brutal and merciless treatment of the defeated population.[6]

The date palm facilitated the development of trade and the spread of civilization in Western Asia and North Africa, particularly throughout the Fertile Crescent, the cradle of invention, agriculture and cities, stretching from the Persian Gulf in the east to the Nile Valley in the west. The date palm was so significant that ancient Mesopotamian cultures also described it with the synonyms 'tree of abundance' and 'tree of riches'.[7]

Portable and nutritious, the palm's dried fruit – calorie-rich, with up to 80 per cent sugar content – could easily be carried on long journeys across barren deserts. In desert landscapes oases were vital in providing shelter and sustenance for travellers journeying along caravan routes. Oases themselves were enriched and enlarged through the planting and cultivation of date palms and, combined with irrigation, became critically important in the development and spread of agriculture. Palms provided a cooler and shady microclimate, allowing cereals, fruit and vegetables to be grown. Settled agriculture allowed communities to become sedentary rather than nomadic; in turn, both palm fronds and stems were utilized for the construction of permanent buildings.[8] The eventual result was a new type of urban form, 'the caravan city', in which the surpluses generated, for example, through taxation, were used by rulers and priests and employed in art and architecture to glorify the powerful.[9]

Ancient and surviving oases, renowned for their date palms, include Tabas in Iran, Liwa in Abu Dhabi and both Tayma and Al-Ahsa, the world's largest present-day palm tree oasis, in Saudi Arabia. The most famous of all oases is Palmyra, the celebrated and, following recent and sustained military conflict and destruction, now tragic city in the Syrian Desert. An ancient stopping place for travellers and caravans between Syria and Mesopotamia, the place name has an obscure etymology, perhaps coming from the Semitic word for dates, reaching back more than 3,500 years.

Beyond Western Asia, Phoenician and Carthaginian traders helped the date to migrate around the Mediterranean Sea and it was probably introduced to southern Europe by about the fifth century BCE.

The date palm had immense utility in the ancient world and almost all parts of the plant could be put to multiple practical uses.[10] Wine from the fermented sap of the plant, for instance, was not simply for drinking: describing a method of mummification, which he witnessed during a visit to Egypt in around 454 BCE, the Greek

A Western view of the utility of the date palm, c. 1840.

historian Herodotus noted how once a body was eviscerated during the embalming process, the cavity was cleansed with palm wine before being filled with myrrh and other spices.[11] Strabo, a Greek geographer and historian who died about a decade before Jesus, wrote of how in Babylonia the date-palm provided:

> Bread, wine, vinegar, and meal; all kinds of woven articles are also procured from it. Braziers use the stones of the fruit instead of charcoal. When softened by being soaked in water, they are food for fattening oxen and sheep. It is said that there is a Persian song in which are reckoned up 360 useful properties of the palm.[12]

The aesthetic qualities of the date palm were also realized. It was a valuable feature providing structure and shade in early garden and landscape design and was presumably used in the fabled (and perhaps mythical) Hanging Gardens of Babylon. The esteem and value given to the date palm by Sumerians, Assyrians, Babylonians and Egyptians is clear from surviving texts, illustrations, pottery and sculptures.[13] The date palm was portrayed in a wide range of ancient decorative arts

Palm-tree design on an unknown object with handle, perhaps a weight, from the Persian Gulf region or southern Iran, early bronze age.

Vase with overlapping pattern and three bands of palm trees, from the Persian Gulf region or southern Iran. c. 3,000–2,500 BCE.

from the Middle East and Africa (many now captured and interpreted in the great Western museums and galleries) and it was sometimes reproduced in abstracted form in classical architecture.

The Mystical Palm

The economic and social importance of the date palm for the Middle East's ancient civilizations led to it assuming a range of sacred and symbolic meanings, particularly of fecundity and fruitfulness. For example, for Semites living in Mesopotamia, within the Fertile

Crescent, it was an emblem of fertility and was associated with a number of deities including Ishtar, the goddess of war and sexual love and a fertility symbol sometimes called the Lady of the Date Clusters. The goddesses Mylitta in Mesopotamia and Astarte in Phoenicia were represented by a female date palm.[14] As a symbolic and sacred tree of the Arabs, the date palm is a contender as the Tree of Life and the tree in the Garden of Eden. Alabaster reliefs of Assyrian royalty and gods also show the sacred and divine tree, the stylized and abstracted design most probably originally representing the date palm and date orchard.[15]

A winged supernatural figure and sacred tree portrayed on a Neo-Assyrian relief panel from Mesopotamia, c. 883–859 BCE. The stylized and abstract tree design perhaps references the date palm and irrigated date orchard.

Palm fronds were used in ancient Greece as a symbol carried by the winged goddess Νικη (Nike) – the Greek word for victory. Coins and mosaics show the goddess carrying a palm frond over her shoulder; victorious athletes were rewarded with a palm frond and it was also carried in processions marking military victories. Adopted and adapted by the ancient Romans, Nike became the Roman goddess Victoria, who again was often portrayed carrying a long palm frond as a symbol of victory. (The name Nike has leapt across millennia to form the brand of the multinational sports clothing and footwear company.)

Date palms became significant early in the history of major religions including Christianity, Islam and Judaism.[16] In Judaism the palm represents virtues such as righteousness, honour, grace and elegance as well as being a symbol of both peace and plenty and of Jerusalem; palm fronds were carried in important religious festivals. There are more than thirty references to the palm in the Bible, including the use of palms in the decoration of the Temple of Solomon and of palm branches to welcome Christ into Jerusalem, and the description of Jericho as 'the city of palm trees'. Lines from the lyrical Song of Songs employ the palm as a metaphor in a celebration of human love and desire: 'Your stature is like that of the palm, and your breasts like clusters of fruit. I said, "I will climb the palm tree; I will take hold of its fruit"' (Song of Solomon 7:8).

In Islam the palm was entwined in a number of beliefs, including that Muhammad himself created the palm tree, commanding it to spring forth from the earth, and that the palm was the tree of knowledge in the Garden of Eden. The Qur'an contains 26 references to the date palm, sixteen of them praising the palm for being God's bounty, and it is mentioned three hundred times in the Hadith – the words and traditions – of the Prophet.[17] A thirteenth-century Muslim historian, using earlier texts, compared the date palm to humans:

The date palm bears a striking resemblance to humans, in the beauty of its erect and lofty stature, its division in two distinct sexes, male and female, and the property which is peculiar to it of being fecundated by a sort of copulation. If its head is cut off, it dies. Its flowers have an extraordinary spermatic odor.[18]

Nineteenth-century Western accounts, including the popular *Thousand and One Nights* and again based on and interpreting far older writings, also noted the importance of the date palm for Islam and the esteem in which it was held:

The date deserves the first place. The Prophet's favourite fruits were fresh dates and water-melons; and he ate them both together. 'Honour,' said he, 'your paternal aunt, the date-palm; for she was created of the earth of which Adam was formed.' It is said that God hath given this tree as a peculiar favour to the Muslims; that He hath decreed all the date-palms in the world to them, and they have accordingly conquered every country in which these trees are found.[19]

There have been borrowings, copyings, appropriations and incorporations of palm legends and stories and their varied meanings across the centuries. The Greek myth of the role of a palm tree in the goddess Leto's birth of the twin gods Apollo and Artemis, for instance, informs both Christian and Islamic accounts of Mary and Jesus.[20] Although there are many variations in detail, the Greek story tells of Leto being impregnated by Zeus and how, harassed by Zeus' furious wife Hera, she then flees. After many misfortunes Leto finds refuge on the island of Delos and chooses a place to give birth next to a stream and under a palm tree. Artemis is born easily, but the labour for Apollo is long and painful, and it is only when Leto leans against or clasps the palm tree that, nourished and helped by it, Apollo is eventually born: 'the old palm tree played midwife for Leto with her poor little leaves.'[21] Subsequently Leto and her twin children held the palm tree sacred.

Apollo with lyre
and palm tree
portrayed on a
terracotta oil flask,
c. 460–450 BCE.

The *Gospel of Pseudo-Matthew*, an apocryphal text deemed untrue and therefore excluded from the canonical New Testament, adopts the Greek myth of Leto. In this story Mary and Joseph escape with the baby Jesus across the desert to Egypt. During the journey Mary rests under a palm tree, although neither she nor Joseph are able to quench their thirst or assuage their hunger. It is then that

> The child Jesus, with a joyful countenance, reposing in the bosom of His mother, said to the palm: O tree, bend thy branches, and refresh my mother with thy fruit. And immediately at these words the palm bent its top down to the very feet of the blessed Mary; and they gathered from it fruit, with which they were all refreshed. And after they had gathered all its fruit, it remained bent down, waiting the order to rise from Him who had commanded it to stoop. Then Jesus said to it: Raise thyself, O palm tree, and be strong, and be the companion of my trees, which are in the paradise of my Father; and open from thy roots a vein of water which has been hid in the earth, and let the waters flow, so that we may be satisfied from thee. And it rose up immediately, and at its root there began to come forth a spring of water exceedingly clear and cool and sparkling.[22]

The following day Jesus says to the palm tree:

> This privilege I give thee, O palm tree, that one of thy branches be carried away by my angels, and planted in the paradise of my Father. And this blessing I will confer upon thee, that it shall be said of all who conquer in any contest, You have attained the palm of victory.[23]

Just as Christians borrowed and adapted the tale from ancient Greece, so early Muslims imitated the Christian story. A section of the Qur'an describes Mary giving birth to Jesus:

The Miracle of the Palm Tree on the Flight to Egypt. Spanish, *c.* 1490–1510.
Between 1919 and 1938 the American newspaper magnate William Randolph
Hearst owned this wooden sculpture; it was sometimes kept at San Simeon,
Hearst's palm-embellished private Xanadu in California.

Thereupon she conceived him, and retired to a far-off place. And when she felt the throes of childbirth she lay down by the trunk of a palm-tree, crying: 'O, would that I had died and passed into oblivion!' But a voice [of Jesus] from below called out to her: 'Do not despair. Your lord has provided a brook that runs at your feet, and if you shake the trunk of this palm-tree it will drop fresh ripe dates in your lap. Therefore eat and drink and rejoice.' (Qu'ran, verse 19. 22–6)

Imitation may be the sincerest form of flattery, and the appropriation and incorporation of the original story indicates the importance of the date palm to economy and society, its symbolic significance, and the desire to elevate emergent beliefs and religions to be on a par with or above the status quo. Indeed, Suleiman Mourad, responsible for tracing of the palm tree miracle back to the Leto myth, argues that the story perhaps originated with a community in West Arabia 'who used to worship a palm tree before converting to Christianity . . . [and for whom] . . . adapting the Leto myth to Mary would have permitted them to keep part of their belief, yet give it a Christian guise'.[24]

The Date Palm Today

Societies and empires fade and die. Civilizations are lost. Such was the fate of the ancient civilizations that domesticated and were then nourished by the date palm. More recent Western societies have looked back at the date homelands and its early civilizations with ambivalence, intrigue and romance: Lord Alfred Tennyson (1809–1892), a British Poet Laureate, captured these emotions in his poem 'You Ask Me, Why, Tho Ill at Ease', which concludes with the words, 'And I will see before I die / The palms and temples of the South' – although the lines might equally apply to other palm homelands.[25]

Across the centuries the date palm, despite repeated disruption and turmoil, continued as an important Middle East food crop with great cultural and symbolic significance. Global date production

Palms flourishing
amid the debris of
ancient Egyptian
civilization: Colossus
of Ramses II in a
Memphis palm grove.

Viewing the
abstracted palmette
capitals of the
partially buried
Temple of Esneh,
Egypt, c. 1900s.
Image from
a lantern slide.

The diversity of dates sold at one of the many date stalls,
Souq Al-Mubarakiya Kuwait City, Kuwait, April 2011.

increased more than fourfold between 1961 and 2014, from 1.85 to
7.60 million metric tons. In 2014 the Middle East and North Africa
were responsible for growing the vast majority of the world's dates,
with Egypt the largest producer, as it had been fifty years before.[26]

Despite the growth in production, contemporary date farming
faces a series of challenges. Yields have fallen because of insect attacks,
diseases, water shortages and decreasing soil quality. Traditional
farming methods have waned and the customary uses of materials such
as the midribs of date palm leaves for roofing and fencing has declined.
There are also emerging and potentially fundamental changes in
dietary habits, with some people preferring new convenience foods
– at times made with palm oil from Southeast Asia – over dates.[27]

Most devastating of all for the modern-day countries that made
up ancient Mesopotamia, the birthplace of the domesticated date
palm, have been the destructive consequences of decades of war,
armed conflict, occupation and political instability for date palms and

the people who tend them. Irrigation systems have been shattered, many orchards obliterated or devastated and farmers killed or driven from their homes and work.[28] Present-day conflict also reaches back to the past: in ancient cities such as Palmyra and Baghdad the archaeological riches of the lost civilizations that once prospered because of the date palm have been looted and destroyed.

four
Western Discovery

ᛞ

D espite the profound disruption following the fall of the
Western Roman Empire, not everything palm-related
from classical antiquity was lost. For one thing, the Romans
bequeathed the word 'palm' to Europe. The Latin *palma* originally
meant palm of the hand; its use in the name 'palm tree' resulted from
the tree's crown of leaves being compared to the shape of a hand with
the fingers spread. The word travelled to Northern Europe early on,
becoming the Old Saxon and the Old High German *palma* and the
Old Norse *palmr*.[1]

The etymology of 'date' for the date palm, *Phoenix dactylifera*, and
its fruit reveals the word travelling along a complicated route, with
the spelling and pronunciation evolving over time. The origin of the
word is probably Arabic or a Semitic language spoken in parts of the
world where date palms were farmed. On adaption by the ancient
Greek, a 'folk-etymological alteration' took place because the date
fruit resembled, and the original word was similar to the ancient
Greek word (δάκτυλος) for a finger; the word was then subsumed
into Latin (the Romans again!) and from there into varieties of French
before jumping the Channel and being used in England by the early
fourteenth century.[2]

There are also relics and artefacts from Greek and Roman civilizations, including, for example, coins, carrying images of the plant
and, especially in the lands bordering the northern Mediterranean,
fragments of palm-related architecture, reliefs, statues and frescoes.

Much of what we know about the ancient palm homelands comes from surviving classical literature.

Travellers in the south of the continent would also have come across real palms. There are just two species of palm native to Europe, both to be found in the coastal areas of the Mediterranean. The European fan palm, *Chamaerops humilis*, clusters around the sea's western shores while the Cretan date palm, *Phoenix theophrasti*, is restricted to a few eastern locations, most notably Val in Crete. Of greater economic and cultural significance, the date palm had been grown in southern Europe for many centuries and, following the Islamic occupation in the eighth century CE of Iberia, in Elche in southern Spain, dates were being cultivated in traditional North African palmeral or irrigated palm groves.

Apart from the word itself, most people living in the north of medieval Europe had fragmentary knowledge of the palm. Few had

Roman Terracotta medallion depicting a successful charioteer with victor's crown and palm branch; made in the Rhône valley, France, late in the 2nd century or early in the 3rd century CE.

seen real palms or visual representations of them. Even so, medieval Europe was not hermetically sealed by time or geography from knowledge of the palm. Christianity became the driving force disseminating knowledge of the plant, albeit often abstracted and fragmentary, around Europe.

The growing power of Christianity brought religious texts, with varied references to the palm.[3] The earliest Old English uses, for example, are in eighth-century religious illuminated manuscripts, including the *Vespasian Psalter* and the *Lindisfarne Gospels*. Palms had an important place in the ritual and ceremony of the church in Anglo-Saxon England, both because their common appearance in heaven imbued 'their appearance on earth with divinity . . . or otherwise serve[d] as a conduit for God's power' and because one tradition asserted that the crucifixion cross was made from a palm tree.[4] Even so, in the north of Europe people involved in Christian liturgy would have been ignorant about the appearance of real palms and those reading or being preached the Bible might have wondered how the righteous would, according to Psalm 92, flourish like the palm tree or why, as described in John's Gospel, palm branches were carried by those celebrating Jesus's entry into Jerusalem.

Particularly in churches close to the Mediterranean, palm motifs were sometimes used as an interior decorative element. The Basilica of Sant'Apollinare Nuovo in Ravenna, Italy, has a mosaic from 576 CE showing a row of date palms behind a procession of virgin martyrs led by the three magi. Another mosaic of circa 1150, from a chapel in Palermo, Sicily, shows another date palm behind Christ entering Jerusalem. There were also rare early attempts to use the palm as an architectural motif in churches in the north of Europe: the chapel in Germigny-des-Prés in the French Loire valley completed circa 806 was decorated with palmettes and stucco reliefs of palms imitating the reliefs in the Temple of Solomon in Jerusalem described in the Old Testament.[5] The palm tree used in religious illustration was increasingly abstracted and stylized and shown as a scaly stem topped by a crown of spurting and feather-like fronds.

Early northern European vision of a palm tree:
a Franco-Flemish parchment leaf of c. 1270.

Scenes from Creation: a date palm shelters Adam and the newly created Eve, who,
formed from Adam's rib, is lifted and blessed by God the Father. Painting
on parchment by the Flemish illuminator Simon Bening, c. 1525–30.

Bartolomeo Montagna, *Saint Justina of Padua*, 1490s, oil on wood. Justina was an early Christian martyr (although portrayed here in 15th-century dress); the palm branch and the sword piercing her breast are symbols of martyrdom.

Christianity took another palm motif – the frond or branch – from classical antiquity and, while retaining how it looked, transformed its meaning. In ancient Greece and Rome the palm branch was a symbol of victory (and latterly also of peace); for Christians it became associated both with Palm Sunday and with martyrdom and the triumph of the soul and faith over flesh and suffering. The 'martyr's palm' entered into medieval religious writing, illustration and carvings: visually it appeared as an abstracted and unopened palm frond or branch.

Texts inspired travel. Journeying beyond the confines of Europe, Christian pilgrims were travelling to the holy land as early as the fourth century and saw palms for themselves and consumed their products. The tradition was established that a returning pilgrim commonly carried home a palm branch fastened to the top of their staff as a treasured memento and evidence of the pilgrimage; they became known as palmers, with the word in use by 1300. Three centuries later Shakespeare had Romeo and Juliet, in the prelude to their first kiss, teasingly manipulate, conflate and confuse the meaning of palm:

ROMEO
If I profane with my unworthiest hand
This holy shrine, the gentle fine is this:
My lips, two blushing pilgrims, ready stand
To smooth that rough touch with a tender kiss.

JULIET
Good pilgrim, you do wrong your hand too much,
Which mannerly devotion shows in this;
For saints have hands that pilgrims' hands do touch,
And palm to palm is holy palmers' kiss.

As to the Elche Palmeral in southern Spain, following Christian reconquest, by 1492 carefully cultivated 'white palms' were being exported from the city for decorative and processional use on Palm Sunday.[6] The tradition continues to the present day, with the Palmeral of Elche now designated a UNESCO World Heritage Site.

The merchants of Venice, Genoa and other European trading places travelled south and east to the Orient and into palm lands ever further afield, encountering other species of palm. As early as the eighth century, and as a result of haphazard and unplanned trading

'Elche the city of Palms – last foothold of the moors in Spain',
photograph by J. Planchard y Cia, 8 April 1867.

within and between continents, the first coconuts from southwest India percolated into Europe, to be wondered about and marvelled at. In the Netherlands and Germany a tradition emerged of turning the shells from what were then the most remote, exotic and tropical of palms into prized and richly decorated cups for both sacred and secular purposes.[7]

European encounters with the palm, especially in the north of the continent, were, then, disconnected and fragmentary before the emergence of early modern Europe from the fifteenth century. From this point, however, there was a gradually developing European understanding of the palm in its native habitat, the diversity of the plant and the uses to which it was put.

Explorers and Travellers

In the fifteenth century Portuguese Christian explorers began a long period of European global exploration. In this 'age of discovery' – a term that wonderfully captures a Eurocentric world view – explorers spearheaded a cavalcade of other Europeans to tropical and subtropical lands: the native homelands of the palm in Africa,

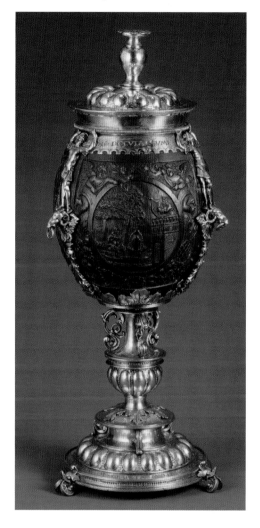

Coconut cup with cover made by the Dutchman Han van Amsterdam, 1533–4. It was believed drinking from such vessels would neutralize poisoned wine; however, the Latin inscription on the bottom rim also warns that 'wine immoderately drunk is harmful as the deadly hemlock'.

the Indies, Southeast Asia and the Americas. Once there, military and missionaries, traders and merchants observed and recorded what they found. Some of them were also natural philosophers, the forerunners of the natural scientists of the nineteenth century, and a genus that played a critical role in the discovery, classification and naming of new plant species.

Printing from movable metal type – another defining characteristic of the early modern period – revolutionized the distribution of knowledge in the West. Travellers' accounts were reproduced in book form and made available to an avid and increasingly wide readership. Europeans were astonished by the nature and societies to be found across the oceans as revealed in the writings of explorers and travellers.[8] The stream of travel literature flowed into the burgeoning knowledge of the Enlightenment, to be consumed by polite society.

The Europeans were more than voyagers, explorers and discoverers. They were also exporters: of people, Christianity, disease, goods used in trade with indigenous peoples, and, in the case of Spaniards making the first European journeys to the Americas, even the date palm. Dates from either mainland Spain or the Canary Islands (a launch point for the long voyage across the Atlantic) reached the

An early Dutch illustration of palm trees and fruit trees on the Gold Coast of Africa, 1602. The text explains the cultivation of the plants and the use of the fruits. The man is engaged in palm wine production.

Caribbean islands and subsequently the mainland of North and South America shortly after the first European visit in 1492.[9] The plant's fruit frequently rotted before harvest in the too-humid Caribbean, but it was more successful when transported to the drier coastal regions of Chile and Peru, by the late sixteenth century, and, by the beginning of the eighteenth century, Baja California in Mexico and the other California immediately to the north. Some of these groves survive and continue to produce ripe dates. The arrival of dates on the west coasts of the Americas is often associated with the building of missions and, in some cases, the actions of specific priests. Father Ugarte was influential in the development of palm groves in Baja California and Father Serra is celebrated for planting the first Californian palm trees in San Diego in 1769 (one plant survived until 1957).[10]

But taking the date palm from Europe to other places was the exception. European travellers to the palm lands began to describe specific palm species and their use by local people. Western plant collectors eagerly hunted for new species of palm, offering names and classifications to the community of natural philosophers. European explorers also transported palms from their native habitats to other parts of the tropical and subtropical world and shipped them back to Europe. Thus began the great migration of palms from their homelands and across the globe. Cumulatively, the plant was to inveigle itself economically and symbolically in all modern societies.

The Coconut

The quintessential palm, *Cocos nucifera*, the coconut, which now grows throughout the tropics, is the most notable example of human-induced palm migration. Most at home on the shores fringing tropical seas, Europeans particularly admired the utility of the palm, which was given its scientific name in the 1750s.

Half a millennium ago there appeared the first European accounts of the coconut in its tropical homelands and detailing how the coconut got its name. Today the dominant and much repeated view, rehearsing a Eurocentric perspective on the world, is that the word derives from Portuguese or Spanish. The most-quoted evidence is from Gonzalo Fernández de Oviedo (1478–1557), who provided one of the early European descriptions of the coconut palm and its uses in an account published in Spanish in 1526. Writing about the Spanish lands in the New World, although also including information from the Asian East Indies, Oviedo explained that the fruit was called a coconut because 'when pulled from the tree the fruit shows a small cavity at the place where the stem was attached, and above it there are two other natural cavities. The fruit looks like a monkey that wheedles or flirts.'[11] The Spanish word *coco* meant face or grimace and *cocar* to make a face, to grimace or to flirt.

Coconut palms on the shore in Saint Lucia.

However, an account from just a year or two earlier suggests that 'coconut' was a European translation of a word that was used by the inhabitants of some islands in the Western Pacific. Antonio Pigafetta (*c.* 1491–1531) was a Venetian explorer and scholar who took part in Ferdinand Magellan's first circumnavigation of the world, between 1519 and 1522. Writing in Italian in March 1521, Pigafetta described how the inhabitants of what are now known as the Mariana Islands and the Philippines used the words *cochi* and *cocho* to talk about what we now call coconuts: the assumption is that the words are translated Italianized versions of the language used by local people. Pigafetta provided a wonderfully detailed description of the plant and its fruit that has contemporary relevance. For example, he wrote that the palm

> bears a fruit, namely, the cocoanut, which is as large as the head or thereabouts. Its outside husk is green and thicker than two fingers. Certain filaments are found in that husk, whence is made cord for binding together their boats. Under that husk there is a hard shell, much thicker than the shell of the walnut, which they burn and make therefrom a powder that is useful to them. Under that shell there is a white marrowy substance one finger in thickness, which they eat fresh with meat and fish as we do bread; and it has a taste resembling the almond. It could be dried and made into bread. There is a clear, sweet water in the middle of that marrowy substance which is very refreshing.[12]

The truth of the linguistic origins of the word 'coconut' may remain hidden. In addition, there continues to be intense debate over where the coconut palm originated and how and when it became endemic throughout the tropical world. A popular nineteenth-century Western view was that the shore-hugging plant 'loves to bend over the rolling surf, and to drop its fruits into the tidal wave. Wafted by the winds and currents over the sea, the nuts float along without losing their germinating power . . . the cocoa-palm has spread its wide domain throughout the whole extent of the tropical zone.'[13] However, coconuts cannot survive in seawater indefinitely – the limit is a little over a hundred days.

It is most likely that two genetically distinct populations of the coconut were native to and originally domesticated on the coasts of southwest India and on Southeast Asian islands. Coconuts from the Indian population have a more oval and angular shape while those from the Pacific are rounder. These coconuts were then spread around the rest of the tropical world not by nature but by humans. There are, though, divergent explanations about who did the transporting and when and especially about how the coconut reached the Pacific coastline of America. In one view, coconuts were moved from their original homelands to other Pacific Ocean and Indian Ocean shorelines long before the age of Western discovery.[14] This analysis proposes that over two millennia ago travellers from the Philippines transported the Southeast Asian coconut to the Pacific coasts of America. The alternative position argues that this never happened and it was left to the Spanish to ferry the plant's fruit from the Philippines and eastward across the Pacific.[15] This may have occurred in 1565, the year the Spanish established the first trade routes with South America by voyaging over the ocean from the west.

The current scientific evidence from coconuts revealing both Indian and Pacific ancestry also indicates that coconuts of the rounder variety were carried along ancient Austronesian trade routes from Southeast Asia to Madagascar and the coast of mainland East Africa. Later, perhaps 1,500 years ago, Arab merchants trading around Indian Ocean coasts took the elongated Indian variety to the shores of East Africa, and there the two varieties interbred. There is, though, a consensus that it was only after 1499 that the coconut began to be spread around the Atlantic coasts of mainland Africa and the Americas and the Caribbean islands. In that year the Portuguese, journeying back from their exploratory voyages to India, introduced the Indian variety of the coconut to the Cape Verde islands, off the

A coconut drupe languishing on the beach at Palm Cove, Queensland, Australia, 2017.

west coast of Africa; over the following decades it was distributed to other tropical shores around the Atlantic.

It took time for 'coco' to be disseminated and accepted among Europeans as the name for a specific palm species. M. Caesar Fredericke (*c.* 1530–1600/1603), a 'merchant of Venice', travelled to India in 1563. Visiting the Portuguese fortified port of Chaul (today long abandoned and ruined) on the west coast of the subcontinent, Fredericke was astounded by the diversity of uses of the coconut and

One of Jean Barbot's annotated illustrations of West African people, with flora and fauna including the oil palm (O) and coconut (Q).

the coconut tree, which he called the 'giagra nut' and the 'Palmer tree'. He recorded:

> In the whole world there is not a tree more profitable and of more goodness then this tree is, neither do men reap so much benefit of any other tree as they do of this, there is not any part of it but serves for some use, and none of it is worthy to be burnt.[16]

Fredericke described how the wood was used to construct ships ('without the mixture of any other tree'), buildings and furniture; the leaves to make sails and mats; the bark for cables and ropes ('better then they that are made of hempe'); the husk of the nut to make oakum for caulking ships' timbers; the shells for spoons and 'other vessels for meat'; and the contents of the actual nuts to extract oil and make wine, sugar and a strong liqueur.[17]

During the seventeenth century the word 'coco' gained widespread European acceptance. The Frenchman Jean Barbot (1655–1712), who worked as a commercial agent in the West African slave trade, wrote vividly of the indigenous utility of 'cocos'. He made two voyages to the Guinea Coast, one in the late 1670s and the other early during the following decade. In an account richly illustrated with his annotated drawings of West African people, flora and fauna, Barbot described how the coconut palm provided Africans with 'meat, drink, clothing, houses, firing and rigging for their ships'.[18] He also thought coconut milk had culinary and medicinal value: 'This milk being boiled with any poultry, rice or other meat, makes a very good broth, and is reckoned very nourishing, and often given to sick persons.'[19]

Recognizing that the knowledge of local people might be applied more broadly and in other ways, Barbot believed that coconuts should be carried in the ships taking slaves across the Atlantic, 'to help their sick men in the passage'.[20] However, it wasn't until the beginning of the Industrial Revolution in Europe that a stronger sense developed that palms and palm products might have a commercial and industrial value beyond tropical lands and in the West itself.

Fredericke and Barbot's praise for the coconut palm's utility was to be reiterated by westerners over the following centuries. A verse much repeated over the last century or so has been that the coconut palm provided 'Clothing, meat, trencher, drink, and can, / Boat, sail, oar, mast, needle – all in one'.[21] In the case of 1920s Ceylon (present-day Sri Lanka), the coconut palm is 'pre-eminently the national tree, the friend of the natives, all of whom share in its benefits . . . There are few gifts of the earth about which so much may be said; its uses are infinite, and to the Sinhalese villager all sufficient.'[22]

Today the coconut's utilitarian importance reaches far beyond its natural habitat. It is one of the world's ten most important crop trees and is of critical value in sustaining many communities. *Cocos* also has a broader cultural significance, ranging through religious symbolism to being a signifier of Western exotic pleasure.

Palm Toddy

From their first palm encounters, the alcohol produced from the plant entranced Europeans. Here are two examples that, despite being separated by three centuries and thousands of miles, suggest similar production methods and European appreciation around the tropics.

Alvise da Cadamosto (*c.* 1432–1488), an Italian explorer and slave trader financed by the Portuguese Prince Henry the Navigator, undertook two journeys to West Africa, in 1455 and 1456. His account of the voyages and discoveries provides one of the earliest European descriptions of both West Africa and the joys of palm wine:

> The liquors of the Negroes are water, milk, and palm wine, which they call mighol, or migwol, which is taken from a tree of the palm tribe, very numerous in this country, somewhat like the date tree, but not the same, and which furnishes this liquor the whole year round. The trees are tapped in two or three places near the root, and from these wounds a brown juice runs out, as thin as skimmed milk, into calabasses that are placed to receive the liquor, which drops but slowly, as one tree will only fill two calabasses from morning till night. This migwol, or palm-wine, is an exceedingly pleasant drink, which intoxicates like wine unless mixed with water. Immediately after it is drawn from the tree it is as sweet as any wine whatever; but the luscious taste goes off more and more as it is kept, and at length it becomes sour. It drinks better than at first after three or four days, as it depurates by keeping, and is not so sweet. I have often drank of it, indeed every day that I remained in the country, and liked it better than the wines of Italy.[23]

In September 1770 Lieutenant James Cook, commanding HMS *Endeavour*, had begun the return journey to Britain of his first great voyage of discovery, which included the earliest recorded European landing on the east coast of Australia. The ship's company included, as official botanist, the outstanding young naturalist Joseph Banks (1743–1820). Banks made varied observations regarding palms and palm wine. Sailing through the Western Pacific, the crew spent three days on the island of Savu, where Banks approvingly wrote of

> The excellence of the Palm wine or Toddy which is drawn from this tree [*Borassus flabellifer*] makes however ample amends for the poorness of the fruit: this is got by cutting the buds which are to produce flowers soon after their appearance and tying under them a small basket made of the leaves of the same tree, into which the liquor drips and must be collected by people who climb the trees for that purpose every morning and evening. This is the common drink of every one upon the Island and a very pleasant one. It was so to us even at first only rather too sweet; its antescorbutick virtues as the fresh unfermented juice of a tree cannot be doubted.[24]

The death of Captain Cook on a Hawaiian beach, portrayed by John Webber, the topographical artist on Cook's final voyage to the Pacific (1776–80). Although fraught with danger, European exploration of tropical lands resulted in greatly increased Western knowledge and understanding of palms.

76

Obtaining palm wine in India. Illustration from a book published in 1689.

Palms and Slavery

The Industrial Revolution led to a profound transformation in how Western societies thought about and used the palm. An illuminating example of these changes concerns one species of palm, *Elaeis guineensis*, the oil palm, and one specific continental region, West Africa.[25]

The oil palm was native to the humid areas of tropical Africa; it was not found elsewhere in the world, although it did have a far less prevalent American cousin. Humans are likely to be the main agency for spreading the oil palm across a vast swathe of Central Africa; most probably the distribution was related to the Arab slave trade and the utility of the species leading to deliberate planting of kernels and tending of individual plants.[26] Europeans first encountered the oil palm when, from the mid-fifteenth century, Portuguese explorers discovered the continent's Atlantic coastline south of the Sahara. Reaching present-day Sierra Leone by 1460, the Gold Coast a decade later and the Congo by 1482, these voyagers provided the first European written references to the oil palm and its uses by Africans: in cooking, for wine, oil and roofing thatch, and in trade.[27]

As the first European arrivals, the Portuguese secured an initial trade monopoly with West Africa. But over the next two centuries other European powers jostled to trade with the indigenous peoples of Africa, to exert their influence and ultimately control. The French were challenging the Portuguese monopoly by the 1530s. Then came the English and Dutch and, in the following century, others, including Scandinavians.

West Africa is a huge continental region. The distance from the Atlantic coast of Senegal in the west to Nigeria's far eastern boundary is on a par with that between Los Angeles and New York City. Its area exceeds that of the European Union. In this homeland, the oil palm thrives on warm and wet lowlands in the zone between rainforest and savannah. Unsurprisingly, given the scale of West Africa, there was considerable variation in the characteristics of the plant itself, in oil palm agriculture and harvesting, in the use of the plant and its products, and in interactions between Africans and Westerners.

West Africans had, of course, been harvesting the fruit of oil palms and extracting and using palm oil since time immemorial. European visitors recorded aspects of this traditional indigenous use. Jean Barbot, working in the slave trade towards the end of the seventeenth century, explained how palm oil was

> of great use to the inhabitants, in several respects, for besides serving to season their meat, fish, etc., and to burn in their lamps to light them at night, it is an excellent ointment against rheumatic pains, winds and colds in the limbs, or other diseases, being applied very warm. The Blacks in general anoint their bodies almost every day, all over with it, which softens and renders their skin smooth and almost shining, and thereby more capable of bearing the intemperances of rain and weather.[28]

Palm oil is obtained from the mesocarp, the middle layer of the fruit's pericarp, the fleshy outer covering surrounding the seed. Because of high carotene levels, the oil is a vibrant reddish colour. In 1725 the great plant collector Hans Sloane (1660–1753), whose collections led to the founding of the British Museum, described the fruit as 'of a Saffron Colour, and smelling something like Violets'.[29] Over time, though, the oil may whiten, thicken and rancidify. In temperate climates the oil is solid at room temperature, making it a valuable stabilizing ingredient in many modern processed foods: spot the palm oil in cakes and biscuits.

A range of methods was used to extract the oil. A common one was to throw the fruit 'into hot-water, then crushing them in wooden mortars, when they are again thrown into hot-water, and the oil obtained by squeezing them in the hands in this state, until it floats on the surface, from which it is skimmed'.[30]

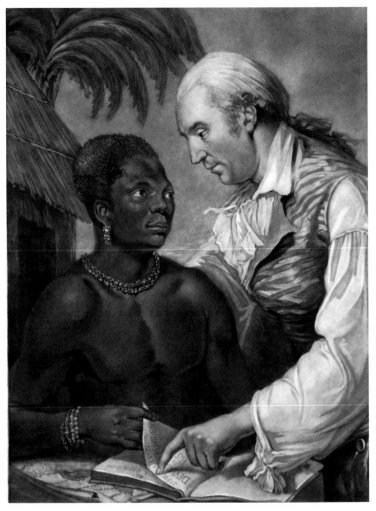

Western discourses – and the associated iconography – of slavery and its abolition also often featured tropical palms. Print made by W. Pyott, *The Benevolent Effects of Abolishing Slavery, or the Planter Instructing his Negro*, 1792, mezzotint on wove paper.

Initially the European trade with West Africa involved bartering salt and manufactured commodities, such as cloth, for gold, ivory ('elephants teeth') and pepper. Then came the development of the triangular transatlantic trade, with European slavers increasingly purchasing palm oil to provision the slave ships crossing the Atlantic.

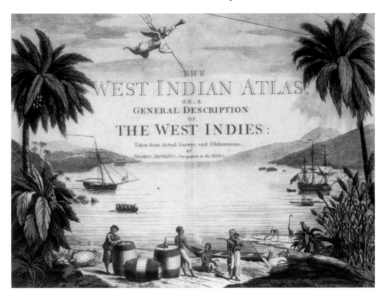

By the time *The West Indian Atlas* was published in 1775, the indigenous peoples and palms of the Caribbean had been supplanted by an influx of human and botanical rivals.

Once across the Atlantic, palm oil was used to enhance the appearance of slaves before sale. Griffith Hughes (1707–1758), writing of Barbados in the mid-eighteenth century, described how

> all the Slaves, brought now from any Part of Africa to this, or any of our neighbouring Islands, are always, before they are brought to Market, anointed all over with Palm Oil, which, for that Purpose, is brought from Guiney: Being thus anointed, their Skins appear sleek and shining.[31]

Some of this oil also found its way to Europe. On 21 June 1785, six months after the first publication of the newspaper the *Daily Universal Register* (later in the decade it was renamed as *The Times*) carried a notice of a 'sale by candle' (an auction) at Garraway's Coffee House in Exchange Alley, at the financial heart of Britain and its burgeoning empire. The varied goods for sale included forty casks of Carolina and Georgia indigo, twenty casks of pimento and a single cask of palm oil. The cask had been carried from Africa to the Americas, from where, presumably surplus to requirements, it was shipped to Britain.

It was not only slaves and palm oil that were transported from West Africa to the Americas, but the oil palm plant. While visiting Jamaica in the late seventeenth century, Hans Sloane described the plant and its uses in detail, basing his analysis on a tree growing on the Caribbean island. Sloane noted: 'This Tree was brought over with some others from Guinea in Tubs water'd by the Way, and then planted by Colonel Collbeck in his Plantation now belonging to Mr Bernard.'[32] The oil palm had begun its migration out of Africa with, ultimately, dramatic consequences for the flora and fauna of other parts of the tropical world.

By 1800 palm soap being made in London's Soho was proclaimed as a 'new discovery, now in the greatest perfection', for use by the nobility and gentry and 'held in the highest estimation, for softening and bracing the skin against the heat of the sun . . . and in its constant use in the winter season, is found an excellent defence against cold winds and sharp frosty air.'[33] Rich white people, some undoubtedly deriving their wealth from slavery, were unknowingly copying and adapting the way that Africans, including those enslaved on the Caribbean islands, used palm oil.

five
Empire and Utility

꙰

On 1 May 1851 Queen Victoria rode by carriage from her Buckingham Palace residence to nearby Hyde Park to open the Great Exhibition of the Works of Industry of All Nations. Housed in another palace, the remarkable Crystal Palace, the Great Exhibition, whatever the import of the 'all nations' element of the title, functioned to demonstrate Britain's global industrial and commercial superiority. The queen recorded in her journal how on her arrival at the exhibition

> The glimpse through the iron gates of the Transept, the waving palms and flowers, the myriads of people filling the galleries and seats around, together with the flourish of trumpets, as we entered the building, gave a sensation I shall never forget, and I felt much moved.[1]

The opening ceremony, performed in the centre of the building, had a curious vegetative backcloth. A number of exotic palm trees were positioned immediately behind the queen and accompanying dignitaries and, further back still, there was a tall elm tree growing in the park and encased by the iron and glass structure of the palace. The display demonstrated society's triumph over nature and the supreme confidence of the Victorians.

The Crystal Palace was partly defined by the palms it contained. More importantly, by mid-century the palm had assumed a significant place in the national economy and society. It was a design motif used on cloth, carpets and ornaments on show at the exhibition. One silver-plated table ornament described a British perception of its place in the world:

> Asia crowning Britannia, on a pedestal of Indian architecture, with palm trees at the angles, Bassi-relievi of the treaty of Nankin, and views of Calcutta, Cabul and Canton. Figures of Affghan and Chinese captives and a British sepoy. The whole supported by recumbent elephants.[2]

Although the use is now archaic, the word 'palm' itself had come to mean the victory or triumph, the prize, or the award of first place or winner: the exhibition literature was full of praises such as 'the palm of honour', 'the palm of grace and elegance' and even 'the palm of ugliness'.

The palm was also suggestive of a series of ideas, possibilities and promises. In varied guises the plant was associated with a natural

Henry Courtenay Selous, *The Opening of the Great Exhibition by Queen Victoria on 1 May 1851*, oil painting. Both the royal party and the immediate backcloth of palms – 'the prince of plants' – ensured the regal nature of the ceremony.

One of Sophy Moody's romanticized illustrations.

life in distant lands untainted by industrialization and urbanization, ancient civilizations, the mystic Orient and, perhaps most significantly, the Holy Land. Apart from the popular palm books by botanists such as Wallace and Seemann, there were other overtly religious publications placing scientific knowledge of palms in a Christian framework. The year following the Great Exhibition the London-based Religious Tract Society published *The Palm Tribes and Their Varieties*, concluding that in the palm tribe 'Divine benevolence and providence' provided 'all the absolute necessities of life'.[3] In *The Palm Tree* (1864) Sophy Moody provided a scriptural and cultural history of the plant. Writing in the third person, the author concluded her preface by hoping that

> May God's blessing so rest on her little work that pleasant memories of earthly palms may be suggestive to her readers of the Tree of Life – the Palm of Victory which in the eternal Paradise awaits all who, as conquerors through Christ, pass through its gates of pearl.[4]

Illustration of the coconut palm, from Berthold Seemann, *Popular History of the Palms and Their Allies* (1856).

The literature of the Great Exhibition also provided lyrical accounts about the uses of the palm around the world:

> Even to savage man the stately trunks of towering palms furnish the simple yet majestic pillars of his temple, or support the canopy of fan-like leaves that he erects to overshadow the resting-place of his ancestors.[5]

Palms were described as 'the most useful of all aristocracies' in the vegetable world, used for 'almost all the purposes to which a plant can be applied'. The exhibition displayed palms used in varied ways: for ornamental woods, cabinet-making, 'multifarious forms of furniture, cordage, weapons, and walking-sticks, and even woven into articles of clothing', fans and punkhas (the Hindi word for large moving fans), baskets and boxes, artificial flowers, cables and ropes, paper and pasteboard, vegetable hair, toys and carven ornaments, the handles of canes and umbrellas and coir ('equal to hemp in strength, and extensively used for the manufacture of cordage, matting, rugs, and brooms').[6]

The date palm not only provided 'an excellent food for the common people of Egypt', but it was a source of cordage, timber, camel feed, fuel and 'a tenacious hairy sort of fibre' used to cleanse the skin while bathing.[7]

By the time of the exhibition the products of the coconut palm were much used in the West. Coconut oil was an important ingredient in many candles – essential for lighting homes – and the fibrous coir from coconut husks was used to make a burgeoning list of items. In 1852 Thomas Treloar, a leading and innovative 'cocoa nut fibre manufacturer', authored a wonderful piece of self-publicity, *The Prince of Palms*, in which he praised the coconut palm 'as one of the greatest of the many blessings showered down by a bountiful Providence upon the inhabitants of a tropical clime'.[8]

A colonial coconut plantation, unknown tropical location.

Treloar also proclaimed the advantages for Europeans of coconut coir over materials such as horsehair and cotton. It was cheap, hardwearing, versatile and could be mechanically processed in Western factories (his own was in London) into a huge diversity of products, ranging through carpets, brushes and brooms, netting for pheasantries, church hassocks, cordage and string and even nosebags for horses. With imports flooding into Britain, coconuts also assumed popular cultural significance as a fairground game and prize, and a familiar yet still somewhat exotic everyday object.[9]

Lubricating Capitalism

By 1851 palm oil, extracted from *Elaeis guineensis*, was the single most important palm product imported by the West. The palm oil produced by West Africans lubricated – sometimes literally so – the development of capitalism. There were ever more machines to be oiled by it, including those in factories and the steam engines that propelled people across land and sea. It was used in candles to light Western interiors, as a flux for tinplating, and glycerine could be extracted from it for use in cosmetics, foods and pharmaceuticals. Palm oil became the great all-rounder, ubiquitous and general purpose.

Palm oil soap was also on display at the Great Exhibition. The Victorians were proud of soap – not only did it occupy 'one of the most important pages in the history of applied chemistry', but the soaring consumption had also led to the discovery of new materials for its production and new patterns of trade and commerce stretching around the world. With West African palm oil as the exemplar, soap, it was asserted, had 'become the means, as well as the mark of civilization'.[10]

The trade in the oils extracted from *Elaeis guineensis* did indeed have a major impact on West Africa. Palm oil became the region's most significant export. The status quo British stance was that the coming of this 'legitimate trade' helped end illegitimate slavery and the abolition of the transatlantic slave trade. By the 1850s it was commonly accepted that 'The development of the trade in palm oil has contributed largely to the abolition of the iniquitous slave-trade on the west coast of Africa.'[11]

The relationship between slavery and palm oil was complex, and in reality palm oil exports did not replace slavery in a causal fashion. One observer reported in 1823 that 'The people of Old Calabar [in what is now southeast Nigeria] have, for a long period, dealt in the productions of the soil, as also in slaves; and have exported, annually, seven or eight hundred tons of palm oil.'[12] Even after Britain declared slavery in its empire illegal in 1807, and although exports of palm oil were rapidly increasing, in some parts of West Africa slave exports continued to rise.

Following British abolition, what had previously been the apparatus of slavery – the British slavers and ships, the home ports in

Oil palm fruit, Abia, Nigeria, 2017.

Palmae
(Cocoineae)

Elaeis guineensis L.

Illustration of an oil palm from the 19th-century *Köhler's Medicinal Plants.*

Britain and the trading relationships in West Africa – became the apparatus of the palm oil business. The English port city of Liverpool, with its wealth partly built on slavery, was transformed into the most important link in the palm oil chain between Britain and West Africa. Northwest England, at the heart of industrial Britain, both provided the goods, including cloth and salt, used for trade with West Africa and consumed much of the imported palm oil in its developing industries, from soap- and candle-making to tinplating.

The imperial project was associated with a diversity of views about the subjected people and places. Western commentators on West Africa frequently lambasted the supposed 'primitive nature' of the region's palm oil industry, with one British economic historian arguing in the mid-1920s that the

> natives . . . who lived in the Jungle Forest were very back-ward. They lived in small communities in forest clearings, and were at ceaseless war with their neighbours, so that econ-omic progress was impossible . . . all energy and enterprise were sapped by the supremacy of witch doctors and the terrorism of secret societies.[13]

The author continued by acknowledging that 'Strictly speaking there is no palm oil cultivation in West Africa . . . and the industry remains very much what it was a century or more ago – merely a collecting and preparing of sylvan produce.'[14]

The reality was far more complex, with systems of production ranging from oil gained from unattended wild plants, through natural but tended groves of palms, to purpose-planted plantations dedi-cated to the export trade. Indeed, whatever the imperialist ortho-doxy, the West African producers were remarkable in increasing supply of palm oil (and at a later stage palm kernels) in response to burgeoning Western demand.[15] During the nineteenth century there was an extraordinary growth in the export of West African palm oil to Western nations. Imports to Britain, the most important market,

The production of palm oil by West Africans overseen by a white man portrayed in a 1844 French drawing. The scene probably took place close to the coastal city of Whyda (present-day Ouidah in Benin). The artisan production methods are still in use today.

rose from 110 metric tons in 1807 to a peak of 64,200 metric tons in 1895.[16]

Just how was this great export business organized? The 'legitimate trade' that dominated for much of the nineteenth century was divided between African producers and brokers on the land and European traders on the coast. In this pre-colonial period, Africans controlled their own lands. Palm fruit was harvested inland; oil was extracted, bartered for European merchandise, including cloth, salt, tobacco, alcohol and firearms, and then transported to the coast by canoe or 'head-loading' and often using slaves rather than free labour. Brokers and traders provided the essential bridge between the Africans inland and the European ships and companies on the coast. Disputes between the two became known as 'palavers', with its root in the Portuguese for 'word'.

The palm oil business was extraordinary in many respects: the webs of mutual obligation and trust; the system of 'comey' or taxes paid to the brokers by the traders; the development of local trade currencies involving items as diverse as gin, iron bars and cowrie shells; the huge effort and wealth involved; and the manner in which the foundations laid in slavery were applied to the palm oil trade. The transport of oil to the coast required astonishing ingenuity and strength. Porters, making long treks overland, sometimes carried 27 kg (60 lb) of oil on their heads; in some places cask-rolling became a specialized technique; transport by canoe was quicker and far cheaper. The wealthiest brokers controlled large fleets of canoes, each carrying up to 2,400 gallons of oil and propelled by up to forty paddlers.

The trade also had its own cast of idiosyncratic characters, including individual African brokers such as King Eyo of Old Calabar, with his fleet of four hundred oil-transporting canoes.[17] The European masters of the trading vessels, many from Liverpool, were often 'rude, uneducated men'.[18] These latter 'palm-oil ruffians' even spawned a

A rare image of barrels containing palm oil being rolled along the road to be transported to the coast for export from what is now Ghana.

genre of white working-class literature exploring the tensions and ambiguities of working in the palm oil trade.[19]

From the earliest days of the trade, transporting palm oil to Europe or North America was challenging. Merchant ships carrying it were sometimes destroyed by storm or caught up in hostile maritime actions in times of war. In late March 1798, for example, the Liverpool-based ship *Tonyn* came into Plymouth after a voyage, the last legs of which involved carrying 317 slaves from Africa to Santa Cruz (most probably the port on the island of Tenerife), returning to Old Calabar in West Africa to load with 'Palm oil and Elephants' teeth' and then, while sailing to Britain, being captured by a French warship and a week later being recaptured, although by that time only one of *Tonyn's* original crew members remained on board.[20]

Three decades later, the *Beaufort Castle* left her home port of Liverpool on 17 February 1828, sailing to Bonny on the Niger delta. Palm oil brokering, trading and loading could take months and, carrying a cargo of palm oil and ivory, the *Beaufort Castle's* return voyage

Palm oil docking point on the Cross River, Calabar, with wooden barrels of palm oil awaiting canoe transport to the coast, c. 1930–40.

began on 22 August. On 8 October the vessel was wrecked in the middle of the Atlantic, with eight of the original crew of 28 surviving after being adrift on the ocean for four days.[21]

From the mid-nineteenth century technological and commercial developments changed the West African palm oil business. The introduction of steamships eased the daunting nature of palm oil shipping and regular and specialized steamer lines were instituted. However, new technologies led to new specialized oils. Trade was increasingly global in its scope: there were new supplies of oils and fats, from other parts of the world, carried to Europe and North America by larger and faster steamships making use of new ports and innovations such as the 1869 Suez Canal. Petroleum emerged as an important substitute fuel for heating and lighting and was soon established as the world's most important oil commodity. There were new and harder-working mineral oils. Australia emerged as an important source for tallow (made from rendered animal fat), long a rival to palm oil. Hydrogenation led to cheaper oils being used in soap manufacture. Zinc chloride replaced the use of palm oil as a flux for tinning. The place of palm oil in Western economies was diminished, seemingly seriously so, with potentially disastrous consequences for West African palm oil exports.

These travails were partly eased when, during the 1850s, it was discovered that oil with a commercial value could be extracted from palm kernels. Previously, although the kernel was edible and the nuts were sometimes used for beads, they were typically discarded in heaps or at best used as flooring or paving. Extracting oil from kernels (the oil is translucent and colourless and akin to coconut oil) was labour intensive: four hundred nuts needed to be cracked open – usually by women and children – to produce 450 g (1 lb) of kernels.[22]

A European market for unprocessed palm kernels emerged. The first baskets – 4,096 in total – of the kernels were exported from Sierra Leone in 1850. Five years later the figure had increased to 155,000 baskets. West Africans were quick to respond to the new market and one contemporary European commentator remarked,

An Ibo mother and daughter extracting oil from palm kernels, northern Nigeria. 1937.

'who then can say that the native will only work under compulsion.'[23] Palm kernels were exported whole and were mechanically crushed to extract the oil in Europe – Germany was by far the dominant importer – and North America.

It was not until the late nineteenth century that European nations exerted more explicit control over the inland regions of West Africa. From the 1880s European countries scrambled to take control of West Africa and emergent colonialism replaced legitimate trade. European states extended their territorial control ever further inland and vast parcels of West Africa were formed into colonies, each under the control of a single European nation.[24] Nigeria, a creation of British colonialism, became the world's most important provider of palm oil.

Soap and Margarine

From the end of the nineteenth century soap was modernized and reinvented, becoming perhaps the first modern Western consumer product. New manufacturing processes allowed the refining, processing and combining of raw materials and production of massive numbers of identical bars of soap. Tropical palm oils became a major component in the new wonder soaps. Palm kernel oil came from West Africa and copra oil, extracted from the flesh of mature coconuts, was sourced from other tropical lands including the Dutch East Indies and the Pacific islands.

It wasn't simply soap being sold. It was a packaged, branded, advertised and marketed product sold to individuals and families who increasingly adopted the role of consumers with preferences to decide and choices to make. The business environment was a merciless world of invention and experimentation, of rivalry and competition, of takeovers and mergers, of massive investment and bold (and sometimes failed) gambles. But when they were successful, the soap companies made colossal profits.

Two of the earliest and most successful wonder soaps (there were many others) were Sunlight, a laundry soap, first produced in 1884 by the British firm Lever Brothers, and Palmolive, a toilet soap, developed by the U.S. firm B. J. Johnson in 1898. The two soaps were the making of the two firms and both companies subsequently became international in their reach and success: today the American firm is Colgate-Palmolive and the British (and Dutch) company Unilever.

Behind the world of global processes, international companies and new consumer products, were individual capitalists and entrepreneurs. William Hesketh Lever (1851–1925), for example, was the driving force behind the development of Lever Brothers into a prominent British company. In the mid-1880s Lever and his brother moved into soap-making and leased a small soap works in Warrington in northwest England. In 1885 a process of experimentation identified that the ideal formula for his new 'pure' soap was 41.9 per cent palm kernel or copra oil, 24.8 per cent tallow, 23.8 per cent cotton oil, with the balance provided by resin.[25]

Four years later Lever's enterprise had relocated to a new, purpose-built works at Port Sunlight, on the marshy banks of the Mersey estuary in northwest England. Complete, self-contained and built for soap, the soap works were to become the world's largest and included a carefully planned and extraordinary model settlement for the workers and their families. Lever was 'capitalism enlightened strictly in its own interest', although he argued that his interests had much in common with those of the British working class.[26] He did not trust the company's workers with their share of the largesse generated from palm oils and Sunlight soap:

> It would not do you much good if you send it down your throats in the form of bottles of whisky, bags of sweets, or fat geese at Christmas. On the other hand, if you leave the money with me, I shall use it to provide for you everything that makes life pleasant – nice houses, comfortable homes, and healthy recreation.[27]

Some commentators applauded the Port Sunlight model village as a visionary and immense achievement. Alternative voices thought it oppressive and suffocating, at best paternalistic and at worst despotic, and a refined version of the 'patriarchal servitude' bemoaned by Engels seven decades earlier.[28]

The palm oil and kernel trade also became bound up with the grander British attempt to transform West Africa through what became known as the 'three Cs': commerce, Christianity and civilization. The British believed such trade would turn West Africans 'into model Victorians keen to encourage commerce and to buy British

Despite the marketing message, the new soaps such as Sunlight depended on tropical palm oils. Lever Brothers advert, *c.* 1890s.

goods'.[29] There were obvious absurdities: the West African palm oils were critical ingredients in the manufacture of soap in Europe; soap that in turn was exported worldwide, including back to West Africa. As graphically revealed in contemporary advertising images, the branding of soap fetishized whiteness and hygiene, denigrated African history and culture, and legitimated Western values and practices.[30]

Anxious to secure supplies of the tropical palm oils required for the business, in 1909 Lever was invited to establish oil palm plantations in the Belgian Congo. Previously known as the Congo Free State, the territory had been neither free nor a state, but instead was the property of Leopold II (1835–1909), King of the Belgians. Both people and country had been horrendously exploited, with forced labour, murder, amputation and rape used as instruments of repression.[31] The king relinquished control of the territory in 1908, ceding it and its debts to the Belgian state.

Lever was enticed by the prospects. Building on the Port Sunlight model, oil palm plantations were developed out of the natural growth of the forest and established in five separate areas.[32] Each was centred on a new township, one named after Lever himself (Leverville) and the others after members of the new Belgian royal family. Lever's attitudes to the British white working class were readily transferable to the Congolese. Visiting the new plantations in 1912, he wrote in his diary that

> The fact is, the native has few wants, a little salt and a little cloth are his indispensables . . . Twelve months ago he and his people were poor and few in number, and were keen to bring [oil palm] fruit . . . After twelve months or less of selling fruit he is rich and lazy . . . The Palm tree is in these parts the Banking account of the native . . . His bank account is always open when he wants to draw on it.[33]

Lever Brothers and the Belgian government argued that the plantation development was in the best interests of all parties: 'as well as safeguarding the physical well-being and cultural development of the native inhabitants, the Convention [agreement] looked after their economic interests.'[34] The company subsequently gained a reputation as a model employer of Congolese people and its official historian, writing in the 1950s, believed the Congo venture had 'given little return to its shareholders by 1939 but it had given much in the way of education and medical help to the Congo'.[35] In the early twenty-first century, Lever himself continued to be described as 'a good man in Africa'.[36]

The counterview is that Lever's Congo intervention was part of an enduring pattern of colonial exploitation. During the formal colonial period, which ended in 1960, palm oil and palm kernels were extracted by Lever Brothers and its later reincarnation using a system of coercion and forced labour, with plantation workers separated from their families for months at a time; those who refused to labour were frequently imprisoned and, once there, controlled and punished by the use of the chicotte – a heavy hide whip – at least until 1959.[37]

Palm kernel oil, being stable and with excellent keeping qualities, was also increasingly used as an ideal principal ingredient (originally it was tallow) for margarine, 'the poor man's butter'. Although Lever Brothers began making margarine during the First World War, there were other much larger margarine manufacturers, including the Dutch firm Margarine Unie. Realizing that cooperating in sourcing and importing palm oils was commercially sensible, in 1929 the British soap maker and Dutch margarine maker merged to become Unilever.

The Anglo-Dutch company was one of the first modern multinationals. In 1933 its British headquarters opened on the banks of the River Thames in the heart of the City of London. Unilever House, which eight decades after its opening is, externally, largely unaltered, was the built form expression of a new modern company and the coming of age of the soap, margarine and related industries. The exterior ornamentation includes two imposing lamp standards, themselves decorated in bas-relief palm tree motifs by the sculptor

A Herculean African clad in a lion skin and carrying a palm tree challenges two serpents. Detail from early 1930s lamp standard at the entrance to Unilever House on the north bank of the River Thames.

Walter Gilbert (1871–1946), flanking the entrance to the building. Stylized scenes relay what was described at the time as 'the raw-material story of the business administered from Unilever House as the artist conceived it'.[38] This tale of heroic humans in the natural and mythical world is far removed from empire, colonialism and capitalist industrial processes. A Herculean figure clad in a lion skin and carrying a palm tree confronts two serpents; in other scenes naked figures harvest nature's bounty and climb palms, pole a canoe carrying palm fruit and bake raw materials in an oven. The sculptures are an expression of the West's fixation with the noble savage at one with nature. The experience of the company's Belgian Congo oil palm plantation workers was very different.

An Emergent Challenge

Two decades into the twentieth century there appeared the first indications that competition from other parts of the tropical world might challenge the West African palm oil dominance.

The oil palm was first introduced to Southeast Asia in 1848, as the result of Dutch imperialism. Four of the palms from West Africa were sent from the botanic gardens in Amsterdam, at the heart of the Dutch empire, to the botanic gardens at Buitenzorg (now Bogor) in Java. The first colonial hill station, Buitenzorg was the summer residence of the Governor-General of the Dutch East Indies and the botanical gardens there began life in 1817 as an extension to the residence's grounds.

The introduction of the oil palms, which together with other species of palm were used as purely ornamental plants, was part of the expansion and opening-up of the grounds. Six years after the arrival of the palms, the gardens were described as 'the paradise of all gardens' and, half a century on, as 'among the finest in the world'.[39] Here is an early example of palms, with their architectural qualities, being used to create distinctive landscapes; in turn the botanical gardens helped turn Buitenzorg into an away-from-it-all haven for leisure, pleasure and recreation.

Palm Group, Buitenzorg Botanic Gardens, Java, *c.* 1860s or '70s.

As the oil palms multiplied, so some were taken for ornamental landscaping in other parts of the Dutch East Indies. Early in the twentieth century a Belgian agronomist, Adrien Hallet (*c.* 1867–1923), who had previously worked in the Congo, noted that the offspring of the Buitenzorg palms were quicker-growing and fruited better than oil palms in the Congo. Pioneers began to develop the Southeast Asian oil palm industry. The pace of planting – much of which was in specifically designed plantations – was astounding: Sumatra, the earliest substantial producer, had 6,000 ha (14,800 acres) by 1919; just over a decade later there were over 80,000 ha (197,600 acres) combined in Sumatra and Malaya.[40]

Nigeria, though, remained the world's dominant producer, with 43 per cent of the global palm oil and palm kernel output in 1933.[41] Even so, there were emergent fears that the result of the Southeast Asian plantation competition 'would be the elimination of the most important export industry of West Africa'.[42] In the event it was not until the early 1960s that the Asian challenge became a serious threat to the West African position. With old-style colonialism on the decline around the world, the newly independent Malaysia moved quickly to diversify from its traditional tin and rubber industries into palm oil harvested from new industrial-scale plantations. This step marked the beginning of transformative changes to the global palm oil business that have reached into the twenty-first century.

six

Of Tigers, Plantations and Instant Noodles

꙰

An astonishing agricultural revolution is taking place in parts of the tropical world. Rainforest, traditional agricultural practices and indigenous communities are being swept away or fundamentally disrupted by the rapid expansion of plantations of *Elaeis guineensis*, the oil palm. An extreme type of agro-industrial monoculture, vast in scale and radical in character, these plantations of serried ranks of palms have fundamentally transformed landscape, nature and society. Although the revolution is most apparent in two neighbouring Southeast Asian countries Indonesia and Malaysia, which dominate the world's oil palm plantation business, over the last three decades this form of intense agriculture has also expanded rapidly in many other tropical countries: today the sun never sets on oil palm plantations.

Although the oils from *Elaeis guineensis* are frequently described using the collective or catch-all phrase 'palm oil', the plant produces two different types of oil: about 90 per cent of the oil is also known by the everyday name 'palm oil', and is extracted from the flesh of the plant's fruit, while the remainder, palm kernel oil, comes from the kernel or seed within the fruit.

Loved and loathed, the oils are two of the contemporary world's most important and yet controversial plant products. Often hidden from view and yet increasingly omnipresent, the production and use

overleaf: Agro-industrial monoculture: an oil palm plantation, Indonesia, 2015.

of the oils illustrate the reach and complexity of twenty-first-century globalization.[1] Although they will be largely unaware of what they are doing, most people living in the West – and increasingly in other parts of the world – consume the two oils and their derivatives on a daily basis.

Global Flows

In the mid-1960s palm oil production remained focused on West Africa, a part of the continent where the oil palm is native and is historically the major palm oil-exporting region. Nigeria alone accounted for over 40 per cent of global production and, following the pattern established over a century earlier, Europe was the dominant importer, taking 70 per cent of the palm oil traded internationally for use as an ingredient in household products such as soap.

However, in Europe and North America the palm oils were increasingly pressed into new uses. As scientific knowledge of the chemistry of palm oil and palm kernel oil and their derivatives improved and the industries refining, processing and transforming them developed, so it became easier to extract different components of the oils and make new compounds.

The two oils played an important part in the post-war transformation of Western consumer society. They facilitated the reimagining of old consumer products and the invention, at an increasing speed, of new ones. In particular, they were bound up – literally – in the previously unimaginable post-war explosion in the vast range of packaged, processed and convenience foodstuffs, personal hygiene and cosmetic products and household detergents and cleaning goods. The oils and their derivatives are found in fast-moving consumer goods as diverse as washing-up liquid and washing powder; shampoo and lipstick; and packaged bread, cookies and cakes, through chocolate, margarine and ice cream to pizza dough.

These new ways of making, selling and consuming were tied to the rise of the supermarket and convenience store as key elements of what it means to be a Western consumer. A much-repeated assertion, although without easily traceable source research, is that palm oil, used in the collective sense, is in about half of all packaged products (in another version it is 'packaged foods') sold in supermarkets. Certainly supermarket shelves are nowadays laden with products that contain palm oils.

Unsurprisingly, European and North American use of palm oil grew substantially. In the fifty years to 2014, European imports increased sixteenfold to 6.3 million metric tons, while imports by the U.S. increased 47 times to 1,410,000 metric tons.[2] People in the West nowadays consume an average of 10 kg (22 lb) of palm oil each year.[3] However, sweeping changes elsewhere in the global geography of palm oil production, trade, use and consumption overshadow the West's increasing use of the oils. Global production rose a staggering fiftyfold over five decades from the mid-1960s: 1,243,000 metric tons of palm oil were produced in 1964 and 61,453,000 metric tons in 2014.

Processing oil palm fruit for local use, Abia, Nigeria, 2017.

Palm oil accounted for 40 per cent of world vegetable oil production in 2014 and, more significant still, it has become an important global commodity.[4] The relationship between increasing world supply and demand has been mutually reinforcing, one leading to the other and vice versa. In 1964, 50 per cent of palm oil was sold internationally; half a century later, and with production fifty times greater, the figure was 75 per cent. By 2014 it accounted for over 60 per cent of the vegetable oil traded internationally.

Even in the mid-1960s, two relatively new producers in Southeast Asia, Indonesia and Malaysia, had emerged to together contribute one-quarter of the world supply. The speed of change was so rapid that within a decade Malaysia usurped Nigeria's dominant world position. Subsequently, the number of palm oil producers proliferated, especially in Southeast Asia and South and Central America. As world supply soared, both the number of importing countries and volume of oil sold internationally expanded.

The extraordinary transformation, in the first decade and a half of the twenty-first century, was the emergence of Indonesia as the pre-eminent global supplier. In 2014, while Malaysia produced 32 per cent of the world's palm oil, Indonesia produced a remarkable 53 per cent and more than half of the oil traded internationally.

Over the same period there were startling changes in the palm oil trade. Many nations in the tropics, some of them also producers, imported increasing volumes of the oil. Nigeria, where the palm oil exportation story began two centuries earlier, produced 930,000 metric tons in 2014 but imported another 550,000 metric tons. In that year, the largest importer was India (taking 20 per cent of the international trade) followed by the EU (16 per cent) and China (12 per cent), with Pakistan, Bangladesh, Egypt, the USA and Singapore following on as other large importers. Nowadays many emerging economies import palm oil on a massive and rapidly increasing scale.

There has also been a developing and remarkable world shift in the processing, use and consumption of the two palm oils and their derivatives. The traditional Western industrial powerhouses of northern Europe and North America have been challenged and overtaken by countries close to those where palm oil is harvested, particularly Southeast Asia. Apart from the logistic and economic sense of locating processing and production facilities close to raw material sources, Southeast Asia also has populations increasing in size and wealth, growing manufacturing capacity and advanced chemical research capabilities.

Apart from palm oil derivatives sold to Western manufacturing companies, finished consumer products are increasingly produced in Southeast Asia and then exported to the West. Take, for example, a bar of complimentary soap, in the bedroom of a modern hotel in the English city of Leeds. The hotel is part of a large international American chain. The soap is made in China, of ingredients including sodium palmitate, sodium palm kernelate, palmitic acid and glycerin, all derived from oil palm fruit grown in Indonesia or Malaysia.

A bowl of palm oil from Abia, Nigeria, 2017.

This change has been coordinated both by national governments in Southeast Asia and huge integrated global agribusinesses rooted in the region.[5] In 2015 the Singapore-based Wilmar International, for example, controlled 45 per cent of the global palm oil trade and was not only one of the world's largest oil palm plantation owners and refiners, but the 'world's largest processor and merchandiser of palm and lauric oils [from palm kernels and coconuts], as well as largest in edible oils refining and fractionation, oleochemicals, specialty fats and palm biodiesel'.[6] The company's three hundred manufacturing plants are concentrated in Southeast Asia and a global research and development centre in Shanghai is devoted to 'new frontiers in food applications'. With an echo of the shipping companies that served the West Africa-to-Europe palm oil business from the nineteenth century onwards, Wilmar also owns the Raffles Shipping Corporation with a fleet of liquid oil tankers. In another resonance with the past, in 2015 Wilmar's two founders began investing palm oil money in property in the City of London – in a site just a third of a mile from Exchange Alley and the coffee house where the first imported palm oil was being auctioned 230 years earlier.[7]

The Wonder Oil

The increasing global supremacy of the palm oils results from nature, modern alchemy and global capitalism colliding and combining, and then spinning off and accelerating in new and unexpected directions.

But what of the petrochemical, animal fat and vegetable oil alternatives to palm oil and palm kernel oil? Petroleum and animal fats, for example, can provide the major raw materials – the feedstock – for household detergents, and tallow may still be used as an ingredient in bars of soap. But their use has been undermined by repeated oil crises and a belief that renewable raw materials should be used wherever possible, in one case, and animal safety scares combined with religious observances, in the other.

All vegetable oils and fats, such as soybean and coconut, may, like palm oil and palm kernel oil, be applauded for their natural, sustainable, renewable and biodegradable characteristics. However, the two palm oils trounce the others thanks to the unique and powerful combination of bountiful harvests, low cost and utility.

Revealing the interplay between botany and economics, the natural characteristics of the palm include very productive oil palm harvests, enhanced further by plant breeding and industrial plantation agriculture. The oil palm has excellent cropping potential and high oil content, with the flesh of the palm fruits containing 40 per cent oil and the kernels 50 per cent. Yields are up to ten times higher than for other vegetable oil crops: it requires just one-tenth of the land to produce the same amount of palm oil as soybean oil. Less land, fertilizer, energy and labour are needed per unit of oil produced. Low production costs equate to comparatively high profits and low prices. And supplies are seemingly boundlessly expandable.

Apart from fantastic yields and low cost, palm oil and palm kernel oil have wondrous utility: their differing chemical characteristics and possibilities set them apart from almost all other vegetable oils. Over four-fifths of palm oil – from the flesh of the fruit – including its derivatives, is used in food applications. Palm oil is semi-solid at a room temperature of 20°C. When not used in this natural state, the oil is typically separated through the process of fractionation into liquid (palm olein) and solid (palm stearin) portions. Palm stearin does not need to be hydrogenated, that is, hardened, to ensure solidity and stability and can be used to make solid food fats such as margarines and shortenings. Palm olein, in contrast, is typically used as a cooking oil for frying food.

The burgeoning success of palm oil consumption in some low- and medium-income countries results partly from the liberalization of international trade, with the cheaper and better-performing palm oil vanquishing homegrown oils, and dramatic if rarely commented-on changes in dietary and culinary habits. In some of these countries palm oil is used in a straightforward manner, simply as an oil to fry food. In India, because of its cost advantages, palm oil has become the cooking oil of poor families and low-budget hot food retailers; wealthier consumers have maintained their use of traditional oils such as cottonseed and mustard. In 2014 about 80 per cent of the palm oil in India – then the largest importer and second-largest consumer of the oil – was used for frying by households, street food sellers and restaurants.[8]

Palm oil is also an essential ingredient used by manufacturers of processed and convenience foods. Because of its chemical characteristics, and unlike other vegetable oils, palm oil is wonderfully stable. It maintains its essential characteristics both at high temperature and over time. Commercial food products, from potato crisps to doughnuts, can therefore be cooked at a very high temperature and, once packaged, will degrade relatively slowly.

The story of the invention of instant noodles, by Momofuku Ando (1910–2007) in Japan, is an astonishing display of palm oil in the global marketplace and of industrial food production by international companies.[9] In 2014 and with the world's population slightly over 7 billion, over 100 billion portions of instant noodles were eaten around the globe, with over 80 per cent of those produced using palm oil. The freshly made and water-laden noodles are dried through flash-frying in palm oil at a high temperature, the moisture being driven out and replaced with the oil. The resultant instant noodles can sit for months, unchanging, in the warehouse, supermarket or local shop. If sold in the classic cup noodle packet, the cup subsequently doubles as both a cooking vessel – in which the noodles are rehydrated with boiling water – and a serving dish.

Although portrayed in the West as a classic student dietary staple, the consumption of instant noodles is actually concentrated in Southeast Asia. South Korean people eat on average more than seventy portions each year, Indonesians and the Vietnamese more than fifty, the Japanese more than forty and the Chinese more than thirty. But

Palm oil adds the 'instant' to cup noodles: display in a Hong Kong supermarket, 2013.

instant noodles are purchased throughout the world, in such varied nations as Saudi Arabia, the USA, Nigeria and Peru, for example, where annual per capita consumption is 28, thirteen, nine and six packets, respectively.

For some Japanese people instant noodles are the greatest of the nation's many modern inventions.[10] They are celebrated by the Instant Ramen Museum in Osaka, which includes a replica of inventor Momofuku Ando's 1950s back garden 'research shed'.[11]

Both palm oil and palm kernel oil also provide the feedstock for the oleochemicals industries. In these industries – increasingly focused in Southeast Asia – natural oils and fats are broken down into their constituent parts of fatty acids, fatty alcohols, methyl esters, fatty amines and glycerol; these basic building blocks in turn providing the essential elements for many other chemicals.[12]

This modern-day and fast-developing wizardry is the stuff of chemical reactions, carbon atoms and chains, molecules and ionic charges. Of key commercial importance are fatty acids. And here the two palm oils are unique in providing, between them, the fatty acids needed to produce an essential range of chemical products used to make processed foods, personal care goods and household detergents. Palm oil is the richest vegetable source of palmitic acid, while palm kernel oil is the major natural commercial source of lauric and myristic acids.

Modern food technologies allow varied and precise palm oil fractions of great utility to commercial food industries globally. Because in its processed form palm oil is neutral of taste and smell, other flavours and scents can easily be added to products. In 2015 the leading integrated palm oil company, Wilmar International, paraded its range of speciality palm and palm kernel oil-based fats sold to food manufacturers in more than fifty countries. The fats, many of which could be tailor-made for specific markets, could do such wondrous and profitable things as, depending on the ultimate foodstuff, improving flavour release, gloss retention, snappiness, aeration, plasticity and 'resistance to staling'. The fats could also reduce costs when, for example, used to replace the more expensive cocoa butter.[13]

In personal care and cosmetic products, the two oils and their derivatives make the impossible possible. Processed and transformed, they become multi-purpose, working as emulsifiers, preventing oils and water from separating and increasing coverage and spreadability; emollients, soothing, softening and conditioning hair and skin; and thickeners and surfactants, improving viscosity, foaming and cleaning.

The lauric and myristic acids from palm kernels provide valuable raw materials to make the critical surfactants – an abbreviation of 'surface active agents' – in household detergents and personal care products. Surfactants clean: when they interact with water they do the essential job of separating dirt from objects such as clothing, floor, crockery, skin or teeth, and floating the unwanted material away in water. Although coconut and palm kernel oils are essentially similar in chemical composition, the latter is cheaper to produce and has market dominance.

Beyond food, personal care and cosmetic products, and household detergents, the palm oils have inveigled their way into industries as diverse as pharmaceuticals, solvents and lubricants, paints and coatings, printing inks, leather, rubber, plastics and other polymers and metal-working. Countries with ready access to palm oil supplies also have rapidly growing palm oil-based biofuel industries. Although with much political argument about the rights and wrongs of the policy, Europe, too, uses palm oil for its biofuel industries. Typically the oil is made into biodiesel, which in turn is often blended with diesel fuel. Advocates argue that using palm oil as a biofuel reduces the use of fossil fuels and the susceptibility of countries to the ups and downs of the world petroleum market.

The Scourge of Deforestation

In demand terms, then, the two palm oils may be presented as a brilliant natural product, of unrivalled value, used for the benefit of humanity. Palm oil has also dramatically improved the economic prosperity of the big (and poor) producing countries and helped alleviate poverty. It provides direct or indirect employment for an estimated 7 million people in Malaysia and Indonesia, and provides the livelihoods of millions of families, ranging from smallholder farmers and plantation workers, to those involved in transporting, refining, processing and trading activities.

Despite the seemingly wondrous utility of the palm oils, as production and global consumption has increased so, too, has the opprobrium directed at them, particularly by Western ecological and environmental campaigning groups, ethical manufacturers and retailers, and consumers concerned with the rights and wrongs of consuming the oils.[14]

Anger is focused primarily on the consequences of the modern production of palm oils. The indictment – and for some critics production of palm oils is criminal – is clear. Oil palm plantations, often planted illegally, destroy rainforests, endanger their rich biodiversity and damage the lives of local people. The scale of deforestation is great. Indonesia, the dominant palm oil producer, is often singled

The threatened rainforest, Sabah, Borneo, Indonesia, 2012.

out for particular criticism. Between 2000 and 2012 more than 6 million ha (14 million acres) of the country's primary forest were cleared, almost the area of the two EU countries of Belgium and the Netherlands combined, and were for the most part replaced with monoculture plantations.

Half the natural forest on the particularly sensitive Indonesian island of Sumatra was lost between 1985 and 2011. Most symbolic are the threats through habitat loss to the survival of iconic animals such as the Sumatran tiger, pygmy elephant and the orangutan. In 2013 perhaps no more than four hundred tigers, an important 'indicator species' of the well-being of the forest, survived on Sumatra.[15] A widely quoted, graphic (and most likely dubious) measure is that each hour an area of Indonesian forest equating to three hundred football pitches is cleared for oil palm plantations.[16]

There are other related concerns. The Indonesian government appears powerless to stop illegal rainforest destruction, even in protected areas such as the high-profile Tesso Nilo National Park.[17] The removal of lowland rainforest, which often includes ancient and deep peatlands, and its substitution with oil palm plantations, releases carbon and contributes to global warming. The peat, made of partially decomposed vegetable matter built up over thousands of years, may contain almost thirty times the carbon of the forests above. When indirect land use change is taken into account, supposedly green palm oil biofuels may ironically lead to the release of more greenhouse gases than fossil fuels.

Fire, sometimes used deliberately to clear land and sometimes the 'accidental' consequence of draining peatlands, is also bound up with the creation of plantations. In Indonesia in 2015, for example,

Peat fires on the Indonesian island of Sumatra, 24 September 2015.
Pale grey smoke blows from southeast to northwest and the red speckles
indicate burning peat on land once covered by rainforest.

'some of the world's largest fires . . . occurred on drained peatlands, releasing hundreds of years' worth of sequestered carbon, sending pollutants into the atmosphere, and burning for weeks or even months.'[18] In the first nine months of that year, 100,000 fires were detected by satellite in Indonesia, the majority in peatland areas. Astonishingly, in just one three-week period greenhouse gas emissions from Indonesian peat fires exceed the total annual German CO_2 emissions.[19]

The blame game is vicious and complicated, with fingers pointed at everyone and everything from indigenous villagers and small-scale farmers, businesses illegally transforming rainforest into plantations, the Indonesian government, palm oil (and pulpwood) producers and traders, multinational Western companies using palm oils and the consumers of their products.[20]

The replacement of rainforest, and in some places traditional subsistence agriculture, with plantations is often unwanted by local

A destructive forest fire in Riau, Sumatra, Indonesia, 2015.

communities. Oil palm monoculture sweeps away long-established land use and customary and ancestral land entitlements, involve human rights abuses and radically disrupt the lives of local people, forcing them to become plantation workers, at best employing them as wage labourers, and at worst enslaving them.[21] For existing rainforest communities, conservation is more financially valuable than deforestation and also 'promotes social and economic equity because it mainly supports the underprivileged majority of society. Deforestation widens the gap between rich and poor.'[22] There are, however, other positions and possibilities. For example, the focus on the negative impact for indigenous communities ignores the positive consequences on national prosperity and standards of living. And some smallholder palm oil farmers proclaim the success and benefits of switching to the crop for them, their families and their communities.

As pressure increases to curb deforestation and oil palm plantation growth in Indonesia and Malaysia, production is rapidly expanding in other parts of the world, typically through a new form of colonialism, 'agro-colonialism'. For example, in West Africa, and in a move that has been both praised and criticized, Liberia's government has awarded long-term concessions to half a million hectares of land to three multinational palm oil companies, including the Malaysian company Sime Darby.[23]

The palm oil saga also continues in the present-day Democratic Republic of the Congo (DRC; formerly the Congo Free State, the Belgian Congo and, between 1971 and 1997, the Republic of Zaire). Unilever sold its neglected DRC plantations in 2009, almost a century after they had been established by Lever Brothers in the then Belgian Congo, to Feronia Inc., a Canadian agribusiness largely owned by development finance institutions that are in turn funded and controlled by Western governments. Feronia has been criticized for continuing widespread labour and land abuses, seemingly an enduring and endemic feature of the Congolese palm oil industry.[24]

Palm Oil and Politics

Of course not all deforestation results in palm oil plantations, although the ecological and environmental critique of the former is invariably linked to the latter. For many people living in wealthy countries, deforestation and all that it implies has great emotional and political salience as something to be abhorred. This repugnance is readily transferred to palm oil plantations and to palm oil itself, and here it becomes personal. Whether they like it or not, most people living in wealthy countries consume palm oil and its derivatives daily, putting it in and on their bodies and using it throughout their homes. Partial and opaque information severely restricts the ability of, say, supermarket shoppers to know whether the products they purchase contain palm oil. Although they may detest deforestation, they are sometimes unwillingly and sometimes unwittingly complicit in the process. Concerns also emerged in 2016 that palm oil used in foodstuffs and processed at a high temperature might pose 'a particular problem' as a carcinogen – and more so than other vegetable oils and fats. Despite or perhaps because of the reassurances of processed food manufacturers, the health alarm added a further dimension to some consumers' fear and loathing of palm oil.[25]

National and international jurisdictions vary in what is permitted or required in terms of food labelling. Until 2015 palm oil in foods sold in the EU could be hidden under the generic term 'vegetable oil'. There is still no requirement to identify palm oil food use in Australia and New Zealand. In the U.S., in contrast, palm and palm kernel oils are readily identified through the use of common names.

Although there is a widely accepted international system for naming the chemical contents in personal care and beauty products, for most people the resultant nomenclature is not illuminating. Peer at the tiny typeface listing the ingredients of shampoo or bubble bath and the common and critical element in most is sodium lauryl sulfate or sodium laureth sulfate. Both are detergents and surfactants that are usually derived from palm kernel oil.

On the ground: a Malaysian oil palm plantation, 2007.

There are well over two hundred names – common, scientific and technical – for the two oils and their derivatives that might be read on a list of ingredients.[26] Because of 'palm' or 'kernel' embedded in the name, some, such as palmate, palmitate, palmitic acid, palm stearin and sodium kernelate, are easy to guess at.[27] But for other additives it is more difficult: common ingredients, such as cetyl alcohol, isopropyl, steareth, glyceryl or glycerine and cocoa butter equivalent or substitute are commonly but not always made from palm oil. In addition, a palm oil derivative, such as cetyl alcohol, may be used in the manufacturing process although it is not, technically, in the final product and therefore not a listed ingredient. For example, cetearyl olivate in personal care products is proclaimed as being made from olive oil but is also, in part, derived from palm oil. Similarly, the use of 'coco' in a chemical name such as coco glucoside, coco betaine and sodium cocoyl glutamate simply indicates the substance was *first* produced using coconut; nowadays such ingredients are just as likely to be made using palm kernels as coconuts.

To the astonishment and dismay of ethically and environmentally concerned cosmetic and personal care companies and consumers, very few hair and skin care products are free of *Elaeis guineensis* oils.[28]

One expression of the politics of palm oil is the vociferous argument about and with the multinational companies – many with headquarters in wealthy countries – secreting palm oil into thousands of everyday consumer products. Campaigning environmental NGOs such as Greenpeace, the Rainforest Action Network, Palm Oil Investigations, WWF and the Union of Concerned Scientists target internationally renowned companies and global brands such as Nestlé, Kellogg, Heinz, Procter & Gamble, the Hershey company, Starbucks and Pepsi.[29]

Views vary about what should be done, although strategies of campaigning organizations mostly focus on research, education,

Scorched earth. Rainforest remnants and a new palm oil plantation near Sungay Hanyu, Borneo, Indonesia, July 2009.

political lobbying and consumer action. Some prefer to work with palm oil companies to change what they do or argue for more explicit labelling to inform consumer choice, sometimes using naming-and-shaming techniques to target recalcitrant companies. In another view, a real commitment to end 'conflict' and 'dirty' palm oil is required with, for example, all supplies traceable to a known plantation and production independently verified as responsible and sustainable. A more stringent position is that palm oil should not be used in consumer products unless it is demonstrably deforestation-free.[30] Others go further still and campaign to boycott products containing the oils or their derivatives and, at the same time, search for more environmentally friendly alternatives.

Arrayed against these campaigners are the producing nations and some of the multinational companies working in the palm oil business. They assert the benefits of the crop.[31] Large palm oil producers and processers herald their own ecologically and ethically responsible plantation practices and business credentials and values. But such companies may also trade in and refine oil from third-party suppliers engaging in illegal activities. Multinational companies, including some producers and some Western food and personal care companies, may be critical and disparaging of 'the green lobby' or may simply refuse to engage in debate or disclose information about, for example, sustainability.[32]

Sustainable Palm Oil?

A potential coming-together of some of these divergent groups and positions is around the production of environmentally and ethically sustainable palm oil. Proponents argue that while it is impossible to avoid palm oil we can at least ensure it is produced to the highest environmental and ethical standards. The Roundtable on Sustainable Palm Oil (RSPO), established in 2004, includes growers, processers, traders, consumer goods manufacturers and retailers, financial institutions and non-governmental environment and development organizations including WWF. The RSPO, working to meet its vision to 'transform markets to make sustainable palm oil the norm',[33] has assiduously developed the globally recognized designation of Certified Sustainable Palm Oil (CSPO).

Despite the RSPO vision, in 2015 less than one-fifth of palm oil produced in the world carried the CSPO designation. And, regardless of the label, the limited demand meant that just half of this production was then purchased as certified sustainable; the balance was sold in the far larger uncertified palm oil market.[34]

The CSPO concept is slippery and illusionary. It covers four different designations.[35] The purest and costliest, akin to single-estate coffee or vineyard-designated wine, is 'identity preserved'. Here the oil can be traced back from retail product through processing and refining to farmer. A second category, 'segregated' CSPO, is also kept physically separate from uncertified supplies throughout the production process, although the oil palm fruits come from different farms and plantations.

'Mass balance' CSPO allows certified and uncertified oils to be mixed together in processing, with the appropriate proportion of the final product labelled CSPO matching the proportion of the input certified oils. If 5 per cent of the fruits being processed come from certified plantations then 5 per cent of the eventual processed oil can be certified as CSPO. The artifice, of course, is that the CSPO oil will be identical in composition to the 95 per cent that remains uncertified.

The GreenPalm 'book and claim' system of designation is still more abstracted and distorted from a reasonable common-sense view of what CSPO should mean. Here manufacturers and retailers purchase certificates for the palm oil they use – whatever the source of the oil – with a payment eventually finding its way back to a CSPO producer. Proponents argue the approach is transitional and encourages the production of physically sustainable oil. In reality, of the more than half of all CSPO using the book-and-claim system in 2015, none was demonstrably sustainable.

Such difficulties are unsurprising. Traceability, the key requirement to evidence sustainability, is immensely difficult given the complexity and scale of the processes involved in producing palm oils and their derivatives. RSPO is also criticized by campaigning groups for being weak and ineffectual and, for example, far too lenient of its producer members, with 'sustainable oil' being neither deforestation- nor conflict-free.[36]

In wealthy countries many leading companies with high-profile brands and reputations have pledged to use only certified sustainable palm oil that is demonstrably deforestation-free.[37] Progress in achieving this commitment in 2016 was uneven. One solution to the traceability quandary is vertical integration of the supply chain, from Western manufacturer to palm oil factory and, ultimately, to known plantations and farmers.[38] While this approach works for palm oil, it is far more difficult to achieve for highly processed palm oil derivatives, which are often purchased from third-party suppliers. The

The industrial scale of the palm oil industry: squeezed oil palm fruits at Langkon Palm Oil Mill, Sabah, Borneo, Malaysia, 2014.

supply lines are typically long and obscure, making it impossible to guarantee a truly sustainable product. Many Western companies then resort to hiding behind the mass balance or book-and-claim CSPO designation.[39]

The challenge is whether the relationship between increasing palm oil production and deforestation can be broken. In theory oil palms might be grown on established agricultural land. The difficulties in doing this in terms of existing rights and landownership patterns are great. And smallholder production of palm oil, while environmentally preferable to plantation production, is associated with yields that may be 60 per cent lower. Another solution proposed as ideal – and both idealistic and unlikely – would be to expand palm oil production on land that has minimal community use, wildlife value or stored carbon.[40]

The search for replacements for the two palm oils is also beset with problems, particularly the enduring issue of finding other oils able to compete on yield, price and utility. Some alternative but lower-yielding vegetable oils use the same lands as oil palm and would lead to higher rates of rainforest loss.

Land cleared of old and low-yielding oil palm plantations, prior to the planting of new young palms, District Kunak, Sabah, Borneo, 2015.

Landscape transformation with rainforest giving way
to oil palm plantations, Costa Rica, 2010.

Despite the devastating environmental and human consequences and related ecological anguish, political protest, direct action and ethical lobbying, replacing rainforest with palm oil plantations is commercially easier, cheaper and more efficient than the alternatives. Global capitalism is fluid, astute, unsentimental and guileful. While it has the capacity to, it will continue to chase the higher profits and cheaper oil to be had by destroying rainforests. The charge of Western hypocrisy is also difficult to refute: in North America, a previous agricultural revolution led to the virgin prairies being replaced with corn and people have transformed the European vegetative landscape over millennia

And away from the torment of some in the wealthy world, ethical and environmentally sensitive products and sourcing have little resonance, meaning or reward for the countries or consumers engaged by issues of price and utility. For the most part the politics and ethics of palm oil are not a concern of the Indian mother as she cooks her family's food, the Korean eating a portion of instant noodles, or the poor American washing his hair or brushing her teeth.

A fan palm exhibited, Singapore, 1860s to '70s.

seven

The Ornamental Palm

ॐ

O nce discovered by the West, palms were heralded for their aesthetic appeal, exotic qualities and striking architectural forms. As ornamental plants, they became key elements in many aspects of garden design and landscape architecture. Gardening itself, the domestication of the plant kingdom, was enriched when specific palm species were tamed, cultivated and put on display.

Western imperialism and empires were accompanied by a burgeoning number of tropical and subtropical gardens. With diverse origins – perhaps private pleasure gardens for the rich and powerful, sometimes food-producing operations, occasionally scientific in purpose – as they developed many were transformed into botanical gardens functioning to enable imperial powers to understand and exploit plants in order to develop commercial agriculture in the tropics and subtropics. The tropical natural world was manipulated and utilized for the purposes of Western empires.[1]

Palms, with their huge commercial potential, became a central element of tropical botanical gardens. Gardens (and empires) vied with each other to build up collections of palm species from around the equator. Economic utility was also leavened by an increasing focus on garden design, and tropical gardens emerged as interesting and enjoyable places to visit, particularly for colonists at leisure and eager to experience a safe version of the tropical natural world. With their visual appeal and architectural qualities, palms became essential elements in the landscaping of botanical gardens, used to provide focal points for promenading visitors to relish and to line paths and avenues. Many of the tropical and subtropical botanical gardens established through imperialism have today become popular twenty-first-century tourist attractions.

The earliest tropical garden founded by Europeans was on the Indian Ocean island of Mauritius, where, in 1735, the first French governor established a private garden to supply fresh food locally and to replenish ships making long ocean voyages. Numerous changes to the garden followed, in its purpose, name and ownership. Past uses, for example, included acclimatizing imported plants: the garden was used as a nursery for both sugar cane and eucalyptus trees. The present-day National Botanical Garden of Mauritius, 'one of the world's best botanical gardens', features a collection of 85 palm species which 'constitute the most important part of the horticultural display and . . . come in an astonishing variety of shapes and forms'.[2]

The British East India Company established 'the Honourable Company's Botanic Garden, Calcutta' in 1786. By the 1860s, and by then transformed into the Royal Botanic Garden, it had become one of the world's largest tropical gardens, carrying out botanical research of commercial and economic benefit for the British colonies in South Asia. Today the Acharya Jagadish Chandra Bose Indian Botanic Garden, 'one of the wonderful relics of the British rule in Kolkata', maintains a palm conservation and research programme and 109 palm species.[3]

Sri Lanka's Royal Botanical Gardens, Peradeniya, have ancient origins pre-dating early nineteenth-century British rule and the development of the gardens as a botanic resource for empire. Palms are an important feature of the present gardens, 'the finest of its kind in Asia', with 2 million visitors a year.[4] The more than two hundred palm species in the collection include the coco de mer palm, *Lodoicea maldivica*, from the Seychelles, which is notable for its giant seed. Three species have been used to line the gardens' principal avenues: Cabbage Palm Avenue (*Roystonea oleracea*), Palmyrah Palm Avenue (*Borassus flabellifer*) and Royal Palm Avenue (*Roystonea regia*).

The most famous South American tropical garden is Jardim Botânico, Rio de Janeiro, Brazil. Lying at the foot of the Corcovado Mountain, and with Rio's iconic statue of Christ the Redeemer to be glimpsed far above, the garden was founded by the Portuguese in 1808 to acclimatize spices imported from the Caribbean. Opened to the public in 1822, today the garden has nine hundred species of palm; a long and spectacular avenue of royal palms planted in the nineteenth century continues to herald visitors from an entrance into the heart of the garden and, in abstracted form, provides the logo of the Jardim Botânico.[5]

Transforming Landscapes

The palm was put to decorative and ornamental use in diverse exterior locations beyond the tropical and subtropical world. In Europe, the world's first botanical garden was established in Italy at the University of Padua in 1545. A European fan palm, *Chamaerops humilis*, was planted there in 1568 and still survives – surely the enduring example of a palm displayed.[6] The port cities of Portugal and Spain, including Lisbon and Malaga, with shipping and trading ties to the tropics, also developed botanical gardens and civic parks where palms, carefully labelled, were frequently given pride of place. Palms continue to contribute to the visual essence of such cities today. El Parque de Málaga, created on reclaimed land at the end of the nineteenth century and planted with palms from Spain's tropical empire, runs along the city's seafront. Lisbon's magnificent tropical and subtropical gardens include the Jardim Botânico Tropical and the similarly palm-laden Jardim Botânico da Universidade de Lisboa. Both gardens were part of an important university research activity seeking to record and exploit colonial Portugal's tropical plants: on its 1906 opening the tropical garden was called simply the Jardim Colonial.

The indigenous vegetation of the European coasts fringing the Mediterranean is adapted to survive in a dry, often hot and relatively inhospitable environment. Early photographs of what was to become

105 NICE. — *Le Palais de la Jetée-Promenade et la Promenade des Anglais*

Despite the palms and exotic architecture, visitors to Nice in the early
twentieth-century still resisted the allure of sun. Postcard sent in 1912.

the Côte d'Azur – a term coined in 1887 – show a plain landscape of
naked hillsides and scrubby, stunted vegetation. The idea of the Côte
d'Azur – the English use the phrase 'the French Riviera' – from the
belle époque onwards depended on the transformation of the area's
flora into a remarkable and exotic sensory feast.

The palm was the revolutionary change agent. It was uniquely
powerful in providing a tall, vertical and regulated architectural
dimension to exterior landscapes and suggesting the exotic. Palms
had to be imported and then acclimatized: the Count of Vigier (1821–
1894) naturalized the first palm, the Canary Island date palm (*Phoenix
canariensis*) on his Nice estate in 1864. The species was soon to be
the making of the famous Nice seafront avenue, the Promenade des
Anglais; Cannes' equally well-known version, the Promenade de la
Croisette, was planted with the same species in 1871.

On the Côte d'Azur and other seaside resorts around the world
where the plant could thrive, and despite drastic changes in the
holidaymaking experience, including attitudes to the sun, palms

opposite: Reflecting Portugal's colonial past (it was originally called Jardim Colonial),
the Jardim Botánico Tropical, Lisbon, is filled with palms.

135

Promoting the summertime Côte d'Azur . . . palms and sun, sea, sand and sex displayed on a 1955 French railway poster.

became the defining characteristic of the seafront. The emblematic plant provided architectural structure and signalled the transition from the often-humdrum inland to the zone of leisure and pleasure beside the sea.[7] The role of the palm-laden Promenade des Anglais as an iconic place of leisure accentuated the chilling character of the 14 July 2016 terrorist attack on the Nice seafront.

The palm also became a defining characteristic of many of the Côte d'Azur's luxurious and exotic gardens and those on the neighbouring Italian Riviera, from the late nineteenth and early twentieth centuries. By the end of the nineteenth century one tropical garden in Nice featured 125 palm varieties.[8] Typically established by rich foreigners, the gardens often involved dramatic preliminary landscaping work, securing rare and exotic plant species and employing expert gardeners. Villas and grand hotels also proudly displayed their palms, seeming to proclaim, 'We are different, special and exotic.'

As holidaymakers looked to seaside venues further afield, and to tropical coasts, they increasingly encountered palms in their natural environment. The development of Hawaii as a tourist destination in the twentieth century helped ingrain the palm in the holiday consciousness of Americans: 'after Waikiki with its groves of coconut

Boat and palm tree outline at a Hawaiian beach.

palms any serious beach had to have palm trees.'[9] Made and remade over more than a century, today's Waikiki beach is a largely artificial creation. The groves of coconut palms that decorate Waikiki are explained with the delicious mythology that they result from the interactions long ago between a supernatural rooster and royal dynasties; in reality the coconut palm is an imported species.[10] The islands of the Caribbean and, more recently, varied Asian coastlines, have also become tourist destinations, with the palm tree, and particularly the coconut palm, becoming the symbol of a tropical leisure idyll.

American Dreams

More than any other nation, the United States has made the palm both an essential change agent and a plaything. In the southern states, and particularly Florida and California, for over a century palms have been implicated in the radical transformation of natural environments, from, for example, coastal wetlands and inland deserts into new and artificial landscapes. In the process, existing communities, too, have been supplanted. Nowadays palms in the U.S. are used to decorate everything from the homes and pools of the rich, to theme parks, golf courses, hotels and resorts, shopping malls, churches, airports and residential areas. Synonymous with particular American towns and cities, the palm helps enhance the sense, meaning and image of varied places, especially those renowned for leisure and the realization of the American dream.

Palm Springs, the most naturally endowed of American leisure places defined by the palm, is a desert resort city in the Coachella Valley, California. The California fan palm, *Washingtonia filifera* (the genus is named after the nation's first president), thrives in a series of oases in sheltered canyons and ravines created by the San Andreas Fault as it runs through the valley. The fault line brings water to the surface, or just beneath it, to quench the thirst of the native palms; in Palm Springs the water was warm and, from the late nineteenth century, white health and pleasure seekers arrived. At first Palm Springs

Palms complement the extreme engineering of the Hollywood Rip Ride Rockit roller-coaster at Universal Studios, Florida, 2015.

offered the antidote to the urban and modern. Riding or driving out to visit canyons and oases including Indian Canyons (which still contains 'North America's largest natural fan palm oasis') was a chief pastime.

But just how 'natural' are the palms growing in the Coachella Valley oases? Historically, the Agua Caliente Band of Cahuilla Indians

Frank Sinatra's Twin Palms estate in Palm Springs, California.

used the palms as a key resource and actively managed the plants through the use of fire, sowing seed and raising seedlings. White Americans, however, refuted Indian palm practices and instead viewed the valley oases from an orthodox Western Orientalist perspective. Palm Springs itself was sometimes called 'Little Araby' or 'Our Araby'. The process was accelerated by the arrival of the movies. By 1920 Palm Springs and its surrounding desert had become the

> headquarters, so to speak, for Algeria, Egypt, Arabia, Palestine, India, Mexico, and a good deal of Turkey, Australia, South America, and sundry other parts of the globe. Wondrous are the sights and sounds the dwellers in Palm

Springs are privileged to see and hear when 'the movies are in town': wondrous the 'stars' that shine in broad daylight on us.[11]

From working in the desert, Hollywood stars began to treat Palm Springs as their playground. It developed into an archetypal mid-twentieth-century hedonistic resort for the rich and famous. The town was also transformed into the epitome of desert modernism, with stripped down, clean, innovative, low-resting and seemingly functional architecture. The palm, with its stark and natural vertical architectural forms, became desert modernism's accomplice.

Behind the transformation of Palm Springs was a rolling conflict, a twentieth-century aftershock from the earlier bloody Indian Wars between the established Indian population and the white incomers, over the use, control and meaning of the palms, springs and canyons. The long-lasting antagonism included, shortly after the Second World War, the city authority's modernization of downtown Palm Springs by 'adding palms and removing Indians – a small-scale municipal case of ethnic cleansing'.[12] In 1949 three hundred *Washingtonia* palms were planted along Palm Canyon Drive with an accompanying irrigation and lighting system to sustain and illuminate the palms.

The drive and its decorative palms became the retail and entertainment heart of the city. By 2016 there were over a thousand palms on the drive, their skirts of dead fronds carefully manicured and the plants additionally illuminated with fairy lights for the festive season. The majority of the city's one hundred golf courses are also adorned with palms. Despite the earlier conflict, the Agua Caliente Band reached an accommodation with municipal and state authorities and is the largest collective landowner in the city.

Apart from being the city of sin, fabulous Las Vegas, Nevada, has become a desert city of palms. The plant typically frames images of the city's iconic welcome sign; it also embellishes numerous Las Vegas hotels and casinos, swimming pools and water parks, and the spine of Las Vegas Boulevard as it runs through the dream city.

The defining coconuts that led to the naming of Palm Beach, Florida, were a fortuitous and unexpected import. In January 1878 the Spanish cargo vessel *Providencia*, which was carrying twenty thousand Trinidadian coconuts to Spain, grounded on the beach of a Florida barrier island. Taking the coconuts as salvage, the early white inhabitants – they had first settled just six years earlier – attempted, unsuccessfully, to establish coconuts as a cash crop. But the palms were to be the making of the area: the Cocoanut Grove House hotel opened in 1880 and over the following decades the idea of a palm beach at home in the United States enticed vacationers fleeing cold northern winters.[13] By 1916 Palm Beach was 'fantastically rich and idle and gay – and useless, if you like. It is a kind of dream of blazing flower-gardens and allees [sic] of palms.'[14]

Another Florida barrier island and another radically remade landscape, Miami Beach imported architectural palms to ornament many of the city's iconic twentieth-century Art Deco hotels and residences; the dunes backing the actual beach are the home of the less distinguished but indigenous saw palmetto (*Serenoa repens*).

Palms provide a harmonious accompaniment to the Art Deco of Miami Beach, Florida. The Leslie Hotel, Ocean Drive, 2015.

The vast postmodern city of Los Angeles is nowadays landscaped and defined by palms rather than its native trees such as oak and sycamore. Eighteenth-century Franciscan missionaries raised the first of the immigrant palms, sowing Canary Island date palm seeds in the gardens of missions such as Mission San Fernando Rey de España and so securing a supply of fronds for Palm Sunday. The great era of planting began much later, in the 1870s, with the palm (first brought to the city from desert oases in California and Mexico and, in subsequent decades, from other parts of the world) emerging as a major element used in the landscaping of the City of Angels and in place publicizing and marketing. The palm became the symbol for the city as a paradise. Although it was not without dispute – a counterargument was that the palm was an alien imposter – the palm came to sum up the dream and desire for the Los Angeles good life of health, leisure and pleasure in a warm and sunny clime where the cold had been banished.[15] But it was also bound up with far more functional developments in real estate, the railroads, civil engineering projects and even unemployment relief schemes: in a single year, 1931, four hundred unemployed men recruited by the city's forestry division planted more than 25,000 palm trees along 240 km (150 miles) of Los Angeles boulevards.[16]

But palms displayed in unnatural circumstances, without a natural supply of water, depend on regular irrigation. The huge volumes of water required to sustain dream communities and their palms are, in turn, captured and transported by impressive feats of civil engineering. Sin City depends on water from the artificial Lake Mead, created after the completion of the Hoover Dam in 1936; most of the water used in the City of Angels is sourced from hundreds of miles away. The developing Southern United States water and environmental crisis casts doubt on the sustainability of palms displayed away from natural supplies of water. If the faucet were ever closed, the palms would quickly wither.

The Moveable Feast

Another critical feature of the palm is its portability. It can be moved, transported and shifted from one location to another: the palm has become a moveable feast.

Some long-lived individual plants have remarkable life stories. Reputedly the oldest palm tree in Los Angeles, a fan palm, native to California although not to the Los Angeles area, has been moved three times over 150 years: first taken as a sapling from a desert oasis in the late 1850s and used to decorate a street in what was a town of just 5,000 people; three decades later moved to make way for a warehouse and transplanted to sit in front of a new railroad station; finally, shifted again in 1914 to guard the entrance of a new city park, Exposition Park, where it stands today over 30 m (100 ft) tall.[17] The siting in front of Arcade Station, with its vaguely Moorish dome, was most symbolic, seemingly welcoming migrants to the subtropical paradise city.

Further to the north in California, towering Mexican fan palms, *Washingtonia robusta*, transform the exterior of the newspaper publisher William Randolph Hearst's (1863–1951) personal Xanadu, Hearst Castle (also known as San Simeon), high on California's Pacific coast. The palms enhance views of the hilltop property from afar and frame the panoramas seen from the windows and terraces of the mansion. Like so many objects at San Simeon, the palms were appropriated from elsewhere; in this case they survived a catastrophic 1923 fire in Berkeley, the roots were excavated, encased in concrete and the plants shipped by barge from Oakland to Hearst Castle.[18]

Today palms, transportable, convenient, architectural and symbolic, are used to make instant landscape transformations. Drawing on palm catalogues, the architects, landscape designers and their clients are able to specify the species, number and size of palms to be used in real estate projects.

The most magnificent and imposing specimens, used in the most expensive developments where palms have greatest symbolic significance – say, a new casino or hotel in Las Vegas – are frequently sourced by palm brokers. The brokers scour vast areas for palms whose owners are willing to sell, arrange removal and transportation to the new location, perhaps hundreds of miles away, and in the process may recoup ten times the purchase price.

Other palms for landscaping are grown on palm farms. The greatest concentration of palm nurseries in the U.S. is at Homestead, Florida, close to the Everglades.[19] Here palms are grown in massed ranks and often sold according to height: in 2016 a coconut palm, for instance, cost $18 per foot.[20] The compact root system facilitates the transportation of palms internationally and, to lessen the spread of earth-borne disease, palms are often grown in large containers filled with ground coir from coconut fibres or composted pine bark. Florida's palm horticulturalists provide immediate and sometimes disposable landscaping used, for example, to decorate exclusive vacation resorts in the Caribbean or to replace existing palms that have been destroyed in tropical storms or by disease, or that have otherwise outgrown their ornamental usefulness.

There are fashions in palm-planting depending, for example, on contemporary aesthetics, and whether the display priority is for night-time illumination or the casting of daytime shadows. There are trends, too, in the grooming and manicure of palms used for ornamentation: whether the rough outer stem should be smoothed and polished, how the skirt of dead fronds on California fan palms should be trimmed and whether the lower fronds on Canary Island date palms should be removed to produce a pineapple-shaped base to the crown. Such work is hazardous. In southern California in the first decade of the twenty-first century more than a dozen people, many of them from Mexico, died while trimming palms.[21]

Portable palms grown in containers are also used to exoticize colder, northern towns and cities around the globe. The French developed the idea of summertime urban beaches. The first Paris-Plages, adorned with potted palms, opened in 2002; since then the idea has been copied by cities across northern Europe, although palms are

Coconut palms frame the exterior spaces of the Coco Palm Resort, Rodney Bay, Saint Lucia, 2016.

sometimes suggested rather than real: in 2015 the post-industrial Amsterdam Roest beach included symbolic palms made from recycled junk.[22]

Pushing Boundaries

Extraordinarily, a few palm species are hardy enough to prosper in the open air far from the usual palm homelands. At a latitude of almost 50°N, Tresco Abbey Garden on the Isles of Scilly is renowned for and defined by its collection of architectural palms, including the Canary Island date palm (*Phoenix canariensis*), the California fan palm (*Washingtonia filifera*), the Chilean wine palm (*Jubaea chilensis*), the Chusan palm (*Trachycarpus fortunei*), the jelly palm (*Butia capitate*) and the nīkau palm (*Rhopalostylis sapida*). The islands, in the Atlantic Ocean just off the Cornish coast of southwest England, benefit from the asset of the mild and typically benign Gulf Stream climate. The location is usually no colder than the Florida Keys. There are also some natural disadvantages, and high walls and shelter belts of Monterey pine and cypress protect the garden from westerly storms and salt-laden winds. This, though, is gardening on the brink, and in the past gales, hurricanes, snow and sustained freezing temperatures have damaged the garden immensely. Although such extreme weather events are rare, Tresco Abbey Garden only endures because of the determination to repair, restore and replant whenever necessary.[23]

Claiming to be 'the most northerly Palm garden in the world', Lamorran House Gardens on the Cornish mainland boasts 35 species

Exotic plants including palms in the protective environment of Tresco Abbey Garden, Isles of Scilly, 2011.

of palm. Facing the same perils as the Abbey Garden, global warming seems to have sustained the diversity of palms in a manner that would not have been possible when the gardens were founded in the early 1980s.[24]

The single most important palm species used as an ornamental plant in northwest Europe and the northwest of the United States, and capable of being successfully grown in the open further north than any other species, is the cold-tolerant Chusan palm, hailing from cool, misty Chinese highlands. Because of the value of the coarse fibres – used to make brushes, rope, cloth and even raincoats – the palm had been cultivated in Japan and China for a long period. Although first brought to Europe by the German Philipp Franz Balthasar von Siebold (1796–1866), the initial introduction to the Royal Botanic Gardens at Kew in 1836 was unsuccessful because the palm was put in a glasshouse where, ultimately, it failed to prosper.

The great Scottish plant hunter Robert Fortune (1812–1880) had more success, making it clear to European horticulturalists that the Chusan palm was best grown outdoors. In 1849 he sent cultivated specimens of the plant to Britain from Chusan Island (or Zhousan as it is now more properly known) in the East China Sea, close to the Chinese mainland. One was planted at the Royal Botanic Gardens at Kew, where it still grows in the bamboo garden. Queen Victoria planted another of Fortune's Chusan palms on the terrace of Osborne House, her secluded seaside retreat on the Isle of Wight, in May 1851. It survived there until felled in 2003. Plants grown from seed collected by Fortune were auctioned in 1860 and so the palm began to populate gardens around Britain.[25]

Some of the most famous and long-lived examples of the Chusan palm are in the sheltered coastal gardens of Cornwall, the mild-weathered and wild-landscaped extreme southwest of England.[26] The gardens, with benign microclimates, were typically established during the nineteenth century by rich private individuals, some with fortunes accrued from capitalism and empire.

Mature Chusan palms stand sentinel in Trebah Garden,
in a mild and sheltered Cornish coastal valley.

The classic example is the atmospheric Trebah Garden, which was founded in 1838 by Charles Fox, a member of a successful Cornish-based international shipping family. The garden is famous for its trio (now duo) of iconic Chusan palms planted perhaps as early as 1860 and with a height of almost 15 m (49 ft). The southern boundary of the valley garden, at the Helford River, offers views of the entrance to Daphne du Maurier's romantic Frenchman's Creek.

Palms seem to imbue Cornish gardens with mystery and exoticism. Like Trebah, the wonderfully publicized 'Lost Gardens of Heligan', 'the garden restoration of the century', tells a story of the revealing of a 'lost world', with palms once hidden from view in a wild jungle of overgrown vegetation being rediscovered and reclaimed.[27]

The Revenge of Nature

The globalization of palms has gone hand-in-hand with the globalization of the plant's diseases and pests, unwittingly transported around the world and threatening to destroy the palm's architectural majesty.

By the start of the new millennium two invasive insects – the palm borer (from South America) and the red palm weevil (from tropical Asia) – were transported to Europe; within a few years the insects began to devastate the Canary Island date palms that defined the seafront promenades and gardens on the French Riviera.[28] Even in California, a veritable modern palm land, diseases such as Fusarium wilt, pink rot, diamond scale and Ganoderma butt rot attack the plant.

Coconut palms, prized for both their architectural qualities and their economic importance, are also threatened by 'lethal yellowing', the name summing up both the symptoms and consequences of a group of related diseases. Also affecting several dozen other palm species, the diseases are caused by specialized bacteria, phytoplasma, spread by leafhopper and planthopper insects. First identified in the Cayman Islands in 1834, in recent decades and through human

Palms bent and twisted by Hurricane Andrew, 1992, transplanted to embellish the Seuss Landing attraction at Universal Studios, Florida, 2015.

agency the diseases have dispersed to many tropical coastlines. For example, to the alarm of people working in the tourist industry, the Caribbean island of Antigua lost almost half its coconut palms in just three years following the first lethal yellow infestation in 2012.[29] The results of lethal yellowing include the premature shedding of coconuts and the subsequent fall of the crown of palm fronds; the result of this beheading is to leave just the stem of the plant eerily upright.

Coconut palms have more than touristic value and the coconut is a major tropical agricultural product. In this wider context, lethal yellowing has 'devastated coconut plantations in tropical regions of Africa and subtropical regions of the world, causing severe economic

Coconuts, ground provisions and bananas for sale, Castries Market, Saint Lucia, 2016.

Monument dedicated 'to the memory of the civilians and war veterans' who died in the 1935 Labor Day hurricane, Islamorada, Florida Keys, 2015.

hardship and environmental damage'.[30] A significant threat to world coconut production, the epidemic has destroyed at least half of Florida's 1 million and four-fifths of Jamaica's 5 million coconut palms.[31]

Storm, hurricane, cyclone and tsunami can all wreak devastation on the most carefully designed palm displays in idyllic holiday destinations. Particularly traumatic are images of the 2004 Indian Ocean tsunami sweeping away people, palms and the paraphernalia of leisure resorts.

But even palms damaged by hurricanes are sometimes used for unlikely landscaping purposes. Following the theme of the Dr Seuss books, one of the design guidelines used in Seuss Landing, part of the Universal Studios Islands of Adventure theme park in Florida, is the banishment of straight lines. The plants used in the attraction include palms with their tall stems bent at extraordinary angles by Hurricane Andrew of 1992.

To the south of Orlando, Islamorada on the Florida Keys is the home of a dignified memorial to the hundreds who died in the 1935 Labor Day hurricane.[32] Palms surround the memorial and a bas-relief on the monument portrays a turbulent sea and palms bending before a violent wind.

eight
Captive Performer

❈

A s the eighteenth century gave way to the nineteenth, the magnificent vegetative spoils of imperialism were increasingly brought home, to the heart of European empires, for the wonderment and pleasure of Western people. In most of northern Europe, however, the climate was unpropitious. Apart from a few hardy exceptions, palms would wither quickly unless they could be kept in a suitable artificial environment. The solution was the development of extraordinary and startlingly modern glasshouses in which palms and other exotic plants were caged, exhibited but also lovingly safeguarded and nourished. There was a sense, too, that the design of palm houses, conservatories and winter gardens echoed and was inspired by the plant's inherent natural architectural qualities. Glasshouses functioned as botanical theatres, with the tropics the major drama on display and palms the celebrity performers.

The raw materials and new technologies of the industrial age were put to work to create these new structures. The separate and synthetic ecosystems both replicated the essence of the tropics, and its heat, light and water levels, and protected the plants from the dangers of cold, dirty and sooty exteriors. Paradoxically coal, the origin of the layers of soot and clouds of smoke afflicting the great industrial and commercial cities, was also an essential resource for

The filigree lattice of the now unique palm house, Bicton, Devon. The structure followed Loudon's early 19th-century palm house designs.

glasshouses, used in the making of iron and glass and for heating and lighting the structures.

Early in the nineteenth century, the new steam technologies had developed sufficiently to allow the climate of a tropical rainforest to be both simulated and sustained continuously in glasshouses. Cast iron, another improving technology, eventually mostly replaced brick and stone as a construction material and often quick-to-rot wood for structural elements and glazing bars. Cast iron was also used for boilers, pipework, walkways and staircases. It was ideal for prefabrication, with the appropriate number of duplicate elements being cast in foundries, then transported and erected on site. A mid-century innovation was the use of rolled wrought iron, newly developed for shipbuilding, to create high, curved structures with minimal internal support. The desire and ability to build larger and taller glasshouses also helped stimulate innovation in glassmaking.

As befits the world's leading industrial nation, many of the advances in glasshouse design occurred in Britain. The most influential of the early inventors and innovators was the Scottish architect, landscape gardener and horticultural writer John Claudius Loudon (1783–1843). Brilliant on the technicalities of constructing glasshouses, Loudon also fantasized about what the future might hold:

> Perhaps the time may arrive when such artificial climates will not only be stocked with appropriate birds, fishes, and harmless animals, but with examples of the human species from the different countries imitated, habited in their particular costumes and who may serve as gardeners or curators of the different productions.[1]

Loudon designed what was at the time the greatest palm house in the world, built in Hackney, on the then outskirts of London, for the family horticultural firm of Loddiges. George Loddiges (1786–1846) was a leading palm experimenter and disseminator. The Loddiges' used collectors to source plants from around the world, transporting the captives over vast distances in specially designed containers to their Hackney nursery for breeding, and then selling the plants throughout Europe. The palm house, built in 1818, innovatively used new cast-iron and steam technologies and included 'extensive steam apparatus' and a 'beautiful contrivance for imitating rain'. In 1824, a visiting German naturalist thought nothing compared to the building's 'magnificence, convenience and elegance'. He went on to describe

> A dome, eighty feet long and forty feet high, built in the form of a paraboloid, purely of glass, kept together by a delicate but strong frame of small iron ribs . . . In ascending to the upper part of it by an elegant stage thirty feet high, we thence enjoy a scene entirely novel to a native of Europe: the tropical plants of both hemispheres . . . are stretched below our feet; and the prospect is similar to what might be presented on a hill clothed with tropical verdure.[2]

Two years later Loddiges boasted 120 species of palm and, in two decades, 280.[3]

Function and Form

As the century advanced so, too, did the design of palm houses and related structures in Britain. Architects and engineers, innovating eagerly with construction techniques, materials and designs, learnt from each other, sometimes in rivalry and sometimes working together.

Joseph Paxton (1803–1865) emerged as an eminent glasshouse designer while principal gardener at Chatsworth House, the seat of the aristocratic Cavendish family, in England's Peak District. The most notable of his Chatsworth glasshouses was the Great Conservatory or Stove built between 1836 and 1841. Measuring 69 m (227 ft) long, 37 m (123 ft) wide and 21 m (69 ft) high, for a short period it was the largest glass building in the world. Paxton was a glass pioneer

and the Chatsworth glasshouse led to the production of the first
1.2 m (4 ft) sheets of glass. Although cast iron was used for some
load-bearing structural elements, other than glass, wood was the
major construction material, with Paxton devising a unique system
of laminated wood for the ribbed elements and a 'ridge and furrow'
design for the curvilinear roof and walls.

   Paxton's technical innovations resulted in a remarkably striking
building. The contents of the interior were wondrously surreal.
Queen Victoria and Prince Albert visited in 1843, two weeks before
Christmas. At six o'clock in the evening of 10 December the royal
party drove in open carriages through the conservatory, illuminated
by 12,000 lamps, to experience the forest of palms and other tropical plants amid a landscape of crystalline and other rocks, water
features including fountains and pools alive with gold and silver fish,

The wonder
of the Palm House,
Kew, as illustrated in
Berthold Seemann's
*Popular History of the
Palms and their Allies*
(1856).

and exotic birds flying overhead. The stately company was provided with an extraordinary sensory experience, delivered on a dark early winter evening in the north of England. It demonstrated how the rewards of empire and British industry might be used for purely pleasurable purposes.[4]

During the great imperial conflict of the First World War, the Great Stove was unheated and the palms died. The semi-derelict structure was dynamited in 1920.

Paxton's Great Stove was the inspiration for the apotheosis of glasshouse design: the 1848 Palm House in the Royal Botanic Gardens, at Kew in London. The Kew building is nowadays eulogized as iconic and as 'the most important surviving Victorian iron and glass structure in the world'.[5] At 110 m (363 ft) long, 30 m (100 ft) wide and 20 m (66 ft) high, it was significantly larger than the building that inspired it. The result of a design partnership between the architect Decimus Burton (1800–1881) and the Dublin engineer and iron founder Richard Turner (1798–1881), the form of the building followed its function to house, display and nurture a diversity of palms from around the world for purposes of science and pleasure. Function and form in turn made the transparent building into a star performer: set on a plinth in the open, surrounded by lawns, rose gardens and water, the structure continues to astound and intrigue visitors in part because of its grace and delicacy and, in part, by offering glimpses into an enchanted interior.[6]

The two designers made innovative use of developing technologies. Turner proposed both that the structure be made of iron and, applying technologies from shipbuilding, that the curved ribs of the building should be rolled wrought iron rather than cast, so allowing for wide unfettered spans and a wonderfully open and unrestricted interior. Another innovation, for the 16,000 panes of glass cladding the building, was the development of a special green glass made with copper oxide (other possibilities were disregarded as damaging to the plants or impractical). The metalwork was painted a vibrant ultramarine. With a few exceptions – there were palmette decorations on the balusters supporting the cast-iron railings and spiral staircase – the structure was radically unadorned. The building was perhaps the first that resulted from a new relationship between engineering and architecture that was not fully realized for another eight decades and the emergence of international modernism: 'in a sense the Palm House was the first modern structure.'[7]

Despite its brilliance, at first the building was not a complete success. The heating system, with the Italianate campanile chimney at a distance (so as not to impinge on the sight of the palm house) did not work well, and early on the palms did not prosper: some died and others had to be moved elsewhere to safety. Over the following decades many changes were made to the heating and ventilation systems and the building became fully attuned to the needs of palms.

Crystal Palaces, Palm Houses and Winter Gardens

The middle of the nineteenth century was a time for iconic British glasshouses. Three years after the completion of the Palm House at Kew, a few miles to the east, in the centre of London, the Joseph Paxton-designed Crystal Palace opened in 1851. Designed to house the nation's Great Exhibition, the celebrated structure was far more democratic than the Chatsworth Great Stove. Paxton was knighted for his part in the triumphant project.

There was a particularly famous palm in the Loddiges collection that was to link the family firm with Paxton. In the early nineteenth century, one specimen of the 'Fan Palm of the Mauritius' (most probably the magnificent ornamental palm, *Latania loddigesii*, that carries the Loddiges name) was shipped from the then French island in the Indian Ocean, apparently to adorn the Empress Joséphine's exotic gardens at the Château de Malmaison, just outside Paris. The plant then moved to London and in 1814 – at which stage it was 1.5 m (5 ft) tall – was purchased by Loddiges' nursery; over almost four decades it graced the firm's palm house. It prospered in the environment, enjoying a sevenfold increase in height, and perhaps even appeared as one of the potted palms in the Great Exhibition of 1851, in Paxton's Crystal Palace.

The Loddiges enterprise faltered and then closed shortly after the Great Exhibition ended. Joseph Paxton seized the opportunity to purchase three hundred of the nursery's palms for the Crystal Palace, which was by then removed from Hyde Park, remodelled and rebuilt as a commercially orientated education, entertainment and amusement edifice in south London. In the summer of 1854 the huge Loddiges fan palm was moved across the capital from Hackney to Sydenham:

> The tree is now about fifty feet high, and weighs upwards of a ton; it is planted in a box, eight feet square, of solid earth. This ponderous mass . . . was first strongly encased in timber with sufficient iron bracings, and shored up on either side. A carriage of sufficient strength, and weighing seven tons, was then placed underneath, and thus the luxuriant load was drawn through the streets by thirty-two of Messrs. Young-husband's finest horses. The progress of this stupendous plant through the metropolis, and the effect of the broad foliage – sometimes sweeping the three-story windows of the houses – will not easily be forgotten.[8]

In its new home, the Loddiges fan palm was probably the plant described as 'the finest palm-tree in Europe' in an 1854 guide to the Crystal Palace.[9]

The glasshouse included a mammoth 'Nave' used to house various attractions and a large collection of plants. At the 'Tropical End' there were specimen palms, 'one of the most beautiful families in the vegetable kingdom', from around the tropical world.[10] In an example of Victorian theming, between the two sphinxes in the 'Egyptian Court' were sixteen date palms. The Victorians were fascinated by the exoticism of palms. Their use in the Crystal Palace, combined with architectural reproductions from ancient civilizations, created

The Egyptian court of the Crystal Palace from Matthew Digby Wyatt, *Views of the Crystal Palace and Park, Sydenham* (London, 1854).

a strikingly unique atmosphere. The sensory experience of some visitors would at times have been disconcerting: 'the palm-tree end of the building', with its higher temperature, was used as a musical venue, to listen to 'the solemn melody of Körner, the playful Charivari of Zullner, and the latest new polka'.[11]

The Palace's collection of tropical plants, including the Loddiges fan palm, was destroyed in a fire in late December 1866, with the *Illustrated Times* describing the remains as 'a scorched and tangled jungle'.[12] The enormous glasshouse at Sydenham burnt to the ground in 1936.

Although its fame and size made it exceptional, the Crystal Palace was not unusual in being more an amusement and leisure palace than specialist plant house: the common thread uniting the two types of glasshouse and others was the ubiquitous palm.

Dedicated palm houses, designed first and foremost to display and nurture palms, were among the most architecturally striking and iconic of the glasshouses built from the early nineteenth century. Scattered around Europe, the locations were mostly north of the Alps. (The 1870s palm house in Florence's Orto Botanico was one exception.)

Royalty and nobility were behind some of the grandest and most excessive schemes. Most extreme, the megalomaniac Leopold II, King of the Belgians, commissioned the giant carpet of glasshouses – including a palm house – in the park of the Royal Palace of Laeken in north Brussels. The complex also featured a vast winter garden, a 'House of Diana' and a 'Congo House'. The Laeken glasshouses were a product and expression of Leopold's merciless exploitation of the

Carl Blechen, *Palm Grove at Peacock Island in Berlin*, 1832–4, oil on canvas. An Oriental fantasy of a palm house designed for Friedrich Wilhelm III of Prussia, the building included fragments of an Indian temple. It was destroyed by fire in 1880.

people and resources of the inappropriately named Congo Free State. Leopold died in 1909, days after marrying his 26-year-old mistress – both events taking place in the Laeken palm house. Still part of the official home of the Belgian royal family, the glasshouses are open to the public for three weeks each year.

Botanical societies and gardens also took immense interest in palms. They were eager to understand and display specimens and so built palm houses to accommodate them. Those in Dublin, Belfast, Edinburgh and Kew in London all came about in this same way. Palm houses frequently evolved over time. The structure built in the Belfast Botanic Gardens between 1839 and 1840 included two curvilinear side wings and a classical-style central section roofed by a shallow dome. A wonderfully curvaceous and taller dome replaced the far-too-low central section in 1852.[13] Richard Turner of Kew fame was also heavily involved in the design and development of the iconic curvilinear range of wrought-iron glasshouses in what is now the National Botanic Gardens of Ireland. Beginning in 1843, the series of connected structures was built in a piecemeal fashion over a quarter of a century.[14] The purpose of the tallest central glasshouse – to house palms – was signalled by the external palmette decorations. The palms

Restored 2002 4. Great Palm House, Dublin, originally opened in 1884; the prefabricated structure was made in Scotland and shipped across the Irish Sea.

Palmenhaus Schönbrunn, Vienna, Austria, July 2006. The 1882 building
was severely damaged in 1945, towards the end of the Second World War,
with some palms dying; the Palmenhaus reopened in 1953.

quickly outgrew their home and were rehoused in a new structure
in the early 1860s. Being unstable, the building collapsed after two
decades. In turn, in 1884 the much taller, at 20 m (65 ft), Great Palm
House opened. The palms' new home of cast-iron columns and
timber-framed glass was prefabricated in Paisley near Glasgow and
shipped in sections across the Irish Sea from Scotland to Dublin.[15]

Many Germans had a particular fascination for palms, and remarkable edifices to accommodate them were built in Bonn, Dresden,
Herrenhausen in Hanover, Magdeburg, Munich and, of course, Berlin.
Following in the tradition of the multi-purpose winter garden, Frank-
furt's Palmengarten – palm garden – combined amusement venue
with palm house. The 'incomparable magic' of the Palmengarten
flowed from 'that phantasmagoria of the captured Orient, which
was incorporated in the Great Palm House from the very start'.[16] And
yet as a private enterprise it needed to entertain and make money.
Incongruously, in 1890 the venue – although not the palm house
proper – hosted 'Buffalo Bill's' Wild West Show, with a cast including
72 American Indians.[17] Unconstrained by the need for a profit, Ludwig

11 of Bavaria fashioned an exotically themed garden, rich with palms, which was contained in a vaulted glass and iron conservatory, 70 m (230 ft) long, built on the roof of the royal residence in Munich and completed in 1871.[18]

Palms were also put on show in countries to the east of Germany and palm houses were built in Krakow, Warsaw, Vienna and, in 1899, St Petersburg, Russia. The 'Big Palm Greenhouse', almost 24 m (80 ft) tall, in what is now known as the Peter the Great Botanical Garden, had the daunting task of protecting its inhabitants from St Petersburg's notorious dark, snowy and icy continental winters. The palm house succeeded for over four decades but was then destroyed, along with most of the palms, in the bitter nine hundred-day-long siege of Leningrad (as the city was then called), which began in September 1941. In a remarkable indication of the importance the Soviets placed on palms, despite the horrors of the battle, some of the most magnificent specimens were rescued and taken to the city's hospitals; there they survived and were subsequently returned to the rebuilt palm house in 1949.[19]

Palm houses needed to be high – and therefore made a great impression on visitors – to accommodate the height of the tallest palms. It was easy to get the calculation wrong. The 1832 palm house in the Royal Botanic Garden in Edinburgh was too low – at a height of 14 m (46 ft) – and wine and sago palms 'periodically sent their leaves through the roof'.[20] One wine palm, 12 m (41 ft) high, was ejected from the palm house and replanted in open ground; it did not survive beyond the following Scottish October.

A second Edinburgh palm house, 21 m (69 ft) tall, was built next to the older structure and opened in 1858. In a realization of Loudon's fantasy of four decades earlier, that 'the human species [as well as palms] from the different countries imitated' should be on display, one Scottish newspaper acclaimed that:

The tropical aspect of this house is heightened by the fact that the man in attendance upon the visitors is a *bone fide*

African. The presence of such a man gives a consistency to the scene; and, besides, it is found that a native of the sunny climes, where the palm trees grow, is better able to stand the high temperature of such a house than one of our pale-faced race.[21]

The older of the two Edinburgh palm buildings continues to house tropical palms, including a cabbage palm (*Sabal bermudana*) about two centuries old, while the newer glasshouse accommodates more temperate palms.

During the late nineteenth century, and particularly in spas and resorts in Europe and North America, the 'winter garden' – the phrase describes the purpose, although sometimes 'conservatory' was used instead – emerged as a significant entertainment venue.

A string of British seaside resorts, especially those with pretensions of respectability, featured winter gardens, and in most palms were an essential exotic element. For example, Blackpool, Bournemouth and Brighton all had versions of the entertainment venue. In Brighton,

A make-believe grotto of palms, fountains and waterfalls: Winter Garden, Brighton Aquarium, portrayed on a card sent in April 1910. The sender writes 'How are you dearies . . . is your garden ready for these plants yet. Don't you wish you were going to the other side of this card tonight?'

The Winter Garden, Nice, *c.* 1890s, before visitors
desired the sunny summer Côte d'Azur.

the aquarium included its own striking winter garden concert hall featuring palms, a fountain and Alhambra-style interior decoration. A short promenade away from the aquarium, the town's newly built 'Marine Palace and Pier' opened its palm-adorned multi-purpose winter gardens in 1911.

The winter garden concept was readily exported. On the Côte d'Azur, the British visitors patronizing the Nice winter season could enjoy the Casino Municipale and its 'tasteful' winter garden, which was used for concerts.

Potted palms also adorned the restaurants, lounges and reception rooms of grand (and not so grand) hotels. Some of the most stylish (and, trying to ape their betters, some not so stylish) hotels included a 'palm court'. Light orchestral music was a typical and important part of the experience: often 'palm court orchestras' performed 'palm court music'. During the first half of the twentieth century, Albert Ketèlbey (1875–1959) was a well-known British composer of light orchestral music. He was famous for melodious works designed to conjure exotic scenes and moods, such as *In a Persian Market* (1920), *In a Chinese Temple Garden* (1923) and *In the Mystic Land of Egypt* (1931). The mood of distant-land kitsch was surely enhanced when concertgoers were surrounded by tropical palms.

By the late nineteenth century there were also private domestic versions of the conservatory designed for wealthier middle-class households living in colder northern climes. The English cartoonist and author Osbert Lancaster (1908–1986) described how palms and giant ferns flourished in his grandfather's conservatory in the early years of the twentieth century. Retaining a deep affection for conservatories, Lancaster thought that,

> To have gathered and selected all the more strikingly un-
> familiar plant-forms, many of them sounding overtones
> of the highest romance – of oases, of desert islands, of the
> Promenade des Anglais – behind glass walls through which
> the reality of nature with all its untidiness, insects and dirt

is clearly visible, and further . . . to have reinforced this Douanier Rousseau-like treatment of the jungle with the addition of water and fish . . . has always seemed among our most civilised achievements.[22]

Survivals and Transformations

Palm houses and their related cousins are a unique building type because of the striking and unusual appearance of the structures, the cultural significance of the plants they contain and the apparent and transparent fragility of both the buildings and their contents. From the outside palm houses offer reflections of light and glimpses of an enchanted interior. From within there is a sense of the realization of an exotic and unobtainable world, while the reality outside, viewed through a wall of glass, is abstracted and remote.

Some palm houses lasted just a few years, while others have survived across centuries. The Loudon-inspired, if not designed, glorious palm house on the Bicton estate in south Devon, England, has stood for at least 170 years, although it has been renewed and restored at various times, most recently in 1986.

Not least because they need to contain and endure a hot and humid environment and the attendant problems of decay and corrosion, palm houses are delicate and precarious structures, requiring continual maintenance and renewal if they are to survive. The prince of palm houses, at Kew, has been both restored and remade. The glass has been replaced on at least three occasions. In the mid-1950s the original wrought-iron glazing bars were cleaned and the entire structure re-glazed. Just three decades later the bars were gravely corroded and a more major restoration, lasting more than three years, took place. The building was emptied of palms – some were felled in the process – dismantled and then rebuilt using 16 km (10 miles) of new glazing bars made, controversially, from stainless steel and 16,000 panes of toughened and curved glass.[23] The visitor experience has also changed: the original Victorian ultramarine painted metalwork was, half a century later, repainted a creamy white and, more recently still, titanium white; palms originally potted now grow in deep beds; and, since the 1980s remaking, there has been a marine aquarium in the basement.

A similar story of the issue of restoration versus replication may be told of the iconic 1902 conservatory in the New York Botanical Garden, modelled on the Kew Palm House. There were violent 'modernizations' in 1938 and 1953, and another major renovation was completed in 1978; a more fundamental remaking completed in 1997 included the original steel glazing bars being replaced with aluminium. Despite the endless transformations and remaking, the conservatory remains 'a stunning example of Victorian-style glasshouse artistry, and a New York City Landmark [and includes] curated displays of

Interior of the Palm House, Royal Botanic Garden, Kew, 2011. The palmette decoration of the spiral staircase – allowing visitors to ascend and view the crowns of the tallest palms – echoes the function of the building.

palms from around the world'.[24] In Dublin the curvilinear range of wrought-iron glasshouses was completely restored in the 1990s, while the nearby Great Palm House, decayed, dangerous and closed to the public in the early 2000s, was dismantled and recreated using new materials and techniques (although some of the original wrought iron was recast).[25]

Apart from the resurrection of old palm houses, the concept has been reimagined for the present day. Occasionally the focus is on planting a grove of living palms within a building. A revealing contemporary story about the fate of such captive palms can be told of the sixteen Mexican fan palms in the Winter Garden Atrium of New York City's Brookfield Place office complex. Located close to the World Trade Center site, when the building opened in 1988 the

The massive stem of a royal palm, *Roystonea regia*, soaring upward in the dome of the Enid A. Haupt Conservatory, New York Botanical Garden, April 2010.

purpose of the palms was to create a 'signature space' to draw visitors. Severely damaged in the 9/11 attacks, the building reopened the following year with new palms from Florida. Although these palms 'came to symbolize new beginnings and change, and so much positivity', they grew quickly and in 2013 were chopped down, turned into mulch and replaced with younger, smaller plants.[26]

Elsewhere, the contemporary focus may not be so much on the palm as a plant family but on tropical rainforest as a biome or ecosystem of which palms are just one component. This is grandiose thinking.

The Montreal Biodôme, opened in 1992 and reusing the city's former Olympic velodrome, is centred on five 'permanent ecosystems'. The most popular, not least because of Montreal's remove from the equator, is a 'reproduction' of a South American tropical rainforest. This 'tribute to the world's most beautiful forest' includes a number of palm species.[27]

More ambitious still is the Eden Project, located in a former Cornish china clay pit in the extreme southwest of England and now the home of the world's largest greenhouse. Opened in 2001, the project is part visitor attraction, part educational initiative and part regional development enterprise. Palms feature in the huge Tropical Biome, 'housing the largest rainforest in captivity', covering 1.56 ha (3.85 acres). Orthodox glasshouse construction methods were eschewed in favour of a structure of hexagonal panels made of tubular steel and plastic film, in part inspired by the geodesic domes popularized by the American designer Buckminster Fuller (1895–1983). The result, like the famed nineteenth-century Palm House at Kew and the original Crystal Palace, is visually exciting and unique. The Tropical Biome, part of the larger complex of domes, is 135 m (443 ft) long and 100 m (328 ft) wide and, at 55 m (180 ft) high, almost twice as tall as Kew's Palm House.[28]

opposite: Mexican fan palms rising to the roof of the Winter Garden atrium of Brookfield Place, New York City, in 2009. The palms had been planted seven years earlier and, four years later and by then too tall, were removed, mulched and replaced.

A view inside the Rainforest Biome, the Eden Project, Cornwall.

The successful palm houses of the nineteenth century depended on design, technology and money. The same three critical conditions will determine the success of the artificial rainforest planned to open in Dubai in 2018. The desert city and emirate is a place of outrageous contemporary real-estate developments, including the artificial Palm Islands. The 0.7-ha (1.7 acre) Dubai Rainforest will be the key family attraction in a U.S. $550 million 'ultra-luxury urban resort destination'.[29] Despite the hostile desert climate, surely inimical to tropical rainforest, the proposal is for an outdoor rainforest on the roof of the building housing the resort's public spaces. In this concept, advanced technologies and biophilic design (rather than houses of glass) are used to protect a fragile rainforest from a hostile alien environment:

> huge jungle canopies provide shade and shelter ... [with the] ... high humidity level mimicking a tropical environment ... created using water stored from condensation.[30]

Sensors will ensure rain does not fall on guests as they enjoy the 'wealth of exotic plants, mist sprays, fish-filled streams [and] an artificial beach.'[31]

Even with the radical new ways of caging palms and other tropical plants used in the Eden Project and proposed for the Dubai Rainforest, there are echoes and reverberations from past great houses of glass. Loudon's 'magnificent, convenient and elegant' Hackney palm house of two centuries ago included a 'beautiful contrivance for imitating rain'. Queen Victoria, visiting Joseph Paxton's Great Stove at stately Chatsworth, experienced a jungle of palms and other tropical plants set in a landscape with pools full of exotic fish with similarly remarkable birds fluttering overhead. *Plus ça change, plus c'est la même chose.*

Jean-Georges Vibert, *Palm Sunday in Spain*, 1873, watercolour. The long-established use of decorative palm fronds and leaves is sustained in many of the world's Catholic and Episcopal denominations.

nine
Abstractions and Fantasies
❦

The abstracted palm as a cultural symbol and signifier became deeply ingrained in modern societies. Simplified and artificial, sometimes two-dimensional, sometimes three, the palm developed as an important design motif used to decorate the interiors of buildings, exterior spaces and diverse objects.

Juan Bautista Villalpando's (1552–1608) illustration of the interior of the most sacred of chambers, the Holy of Holies, in King Solomon's Temple in Jerusalem, was published in 1604; it was to have a lasting impact on interior design and decoration. A Jesuit priest, scholar and architect, Villalpando's depiction was his interpretation of the Prophet Ezekiel's comments about the temple in the Old Testament. It shows the Ark of the Covenant, protective cherubim with wings and cloven feet, and walls decorated with scaly-stemmed palms from which flow feathery fronds; the overall impression is of a divine space within a palm grove.[1]

Villalpando's vision of celestial interior decor, designed by God and with a central role for the palm, was put to multiple uses. In particular, palm trees and fronds become a minor but visually striking element in the interior decoration of European royal palaces, stately homes and churches. In 1665 the English architect John Webb (1611–1672) designed a bedchamber at Greenwich Palace for the British king Charles II, with the opening to the alcove containing the royal bed framed theatrically by palm trees and sweeping palm fronds.[2] Apart from implying the king's divine right to the

One of the palm-tree confessionals, Zwiefalten monastery church, Germany.

decoration, the priapic palms also suggested regal fecundity and sexual union.

Webb's design remained unexecuted, but the stylized palm, echoing Villalpando's concept, was at last realized in the gilded ornamentation on the 1710 rococo organ dominating Louis xiv's royal chapel at Versailles.[3] Three decades later Louis xv continued the use of the palm motif at Versailles in his private bedchamber.

By mid-century the religious, royal and aristocratic use of the palm had spread elsewhere. The 1740s Baroque monastery church at Zwiefalten in southern Germany contains palm tree confessionals conforming to the Villalpando vision. One confessional, portraying the consequences of sin, shows palm trees destroyed; the other, suggesting renewal and penitence, depicts a healthy and sustaining palm grove.[4]

In London, the mid-1750s Palm Room in Spencer House, used as the gentlemen's after-dinner retiring room, drew directly on Webb's design of nine decades earlier and indirectly on Villalpando's 150-year-old fantasy of the Holy of Holies.[5] Here, though, the palm hints at classical architecture, nature and pleasure. The same lineage and date, and similar invented and idealized palms, applied to the rococo walnut Palm Room in the Bayreuth New Palace in Bavaria. The room served as a banqueting hall, where guests would have enjoyed both a visual and culinary feast, and a masonic lodge; the latter use was most appropriate given the importance of Solomon's Temple for freemasons.[6]

As the appeal of the palm broadened it became associated with diverse ideas. Chinoiserie became popular as a European decorative style drawing on design themes from China and suggesting a mysterious and exotic faraway world. Completed in 1764 for the Prussian emperor Frederick the Great, the exterior of the Chinese Teahouse, in Sanssouci Park in Potsdam, Germany, provides a tableau tea party. The sandstone columns supporting the roof of the

Gilded palms as make-believe, decorating the 1764 Chinese Teahouse in Sanssouci Park, Potsdam, Germany.

pavilion serve another purpose: gilded and decorated as rococoesque palm trees, they provide the theatrical set for life-size figures to enjoy the musical tea soiree.[7]

In Britain the most influential use of palms for interior decoration was in Brighton's Royal Pavilion, completed in the early 1820s. As architect for the hedonistic Prince Regent, John Nash's (1752–1835) concern was to produce a fantasy; he drew on an eclectic menagerie of styles and images with palms and palm motifs playing a major role. Cast-iron columns to support roofs and ceilings were decorated as palm trees, the designs sometimes abstract and sometimes uncertain: in one case the stem appears as bamboo, the fronds as palm. Even the columns supporting the kitchen roof, necessary to make a large and open workspace, were embroidered with copper palm leaves.[8] Form followed the function of structural support for the pavilion and the Prince's requirement to transform the building into a confection used to transport those who experienced it to a make-believe and decadent other world. It was 'a sunny pleasure-dome at

John Nash, watercolour illustration of the Great Kitchen with Oriental – and palm – themes, from his 19th-century *Views of the Royal Pavilion.*

Brighton, like a dream of Xanadu, in which a corpulent Kubla could sit in state beneath cast iron columns disguised as palm trees'.[9]

Symbols and Meanings

Varied meanings, including 'victory, peace, heaven, righteousness, sexual fertility, martyrdom and exoticism', became attached to the palm motif.[10] The use of a palm frond to decorate a tomb, for example, symbolized victory over death. As an emblem and symbol the palm has embroidered a vast range of objects, from military medals and flags to tourist coaches and leisure pools. During the Second World War it was even appropriated by German forces fighting in the deserts of North Africa: the Africa Korps emblem was a palm tree with superimposed swastika.

In scale the palm as an architectural signifier and symbol ranges from the minuscule to the colossal. At one extreme, the palmette, the stylized abstraction of the date palm's crown that first appeared in ancient Egypt, was reinvented and reused for modern purposes. In varied forms it became an ornament on Renaissance sculpture, Baroque fountains, Neoclassical architecture, cast-iron Regency railings and balconies, Victorian palm houses and twentieth-century suburban garden gates.[11]

The most dominant contemporary meaning attached to the palm is to signify ideas of the exotic and the pleasurable other. Both in texts and visually the palm has become inveigled in varied fantasies, dreams and fictions; it has become the symbol of make-believe. The palm has become an essential element in the idea of particular types of real and imaginary places. As powerful metaphors, 'what they [palms] mean *is* what they do.'[12]

Palms help define the idea of places such as the Côte d'Azur, the South Seas and California.[13] The work of influential image-makers – including artists, writers and film-makers – has strengthened and intensified palm meanings. The Côte d'Azur's palms seduced the artists Claude Monet, Henri Matisse and Raoul Dufy while the palms

The tropical palm-tree motif has crept into the most unlikely of seaside places. Jaywick Sands on the Thames estuary to the east of London, April 2010. Five years later Jaywick was officially identified as the most deprived neighbourhood in England.

The remains of the Parachute Jump, a relict of Coney Island's great amusement park business, mirrors the form of the more recent artificial palm tree on Coney Island beach, Brooklyn, New York, 2009.

An Impressionist vision of the Italian Riviera: Claude Monet,
Palm Trees at Bordighera, 1884, oil on canvas.

– and women – of French Polynesia similarly beguiled Paul Gauguin.[14] The resulting iconic art subsequently reinforced and developed popular perceptions of the meaning of such palm-rich places.

Since its use in the Brighton Royal Pavilion two centuries ago, the palm has often been used by designers of the modern seaside in the quest to transform the drab and ordinary into exotic other places. Where real palms could not survive, weaving the palm into the design tapestry of colder northern seaside resorts in Europe and North America required the thread to be artificial and emblematic rather than real.[15]

New materials such as fibreglass, metal alloys and plastics have also extended the range of palm tree-based design possibilities to other leisure places, including children's playgrounds, music festivals and theme parks. Most recently 'preserved palm trees' – real palms with 'their organic functions terminated', and component parts removed, embalmed and then reconstructed around a steel

The real made artificial and a shopping affectation. Preserved palm trees used to decorate the Trafford Centre, Manchester, 2016.

core – have spread around the world into restaurants, casino resorts, hotels, shopping malls and the public spaces of office buildings.[16] Whatever the circumstance, the palm tree charade is that we are really somewhere else, somewhere preferable.

The definitive architectural use of the palm is on the coast of Dubai, where the three artificial 'Palm Islands', each in the shape of the date palm, form the world's largest construction project.[17] When completed the Palm Islands, 'iconic mega-projects' with huge luxury seaside residential and leisure complexes, will have added 120 km (74 miles) of beach to Dubai's coastline. This ultimate vision in abstracting the palm and designing the seaside is part of a strategy to transform the emirate into a global tourist destination. The inspiration of the ruler of Dubai, Sheikh Mohammed bin Rashid Al Maktoum, the date palm motif was chosen because the plant was 'one of Dubai's most enduring symbols of life and abundance'; paradoxically, critics voice concerns about the islands' negative ecological and environmental impact and sustainability.[18]

Use of the date palm has other benefits for the project. Not only did the plant's shape, at a suitable scale, allow each of the thousands of new residences their own private beach and access to the sea, it created 'an instantly recognizable symbol for Dubai and . . . brand Dubai'.[19] In this sense the Palm Islands are 'a generic place whose symbolism does not relate to a specific localized culture as date palms are grown all over the Arab world . . . [and are] . . . perfect examples of symbols that became objects'.[20]

For two centuries an architectural symbol used to glamorize and romanticize the Western seaside, the idea of the palm has been recaptured and embraced by Dubai to create a spectacular new form of twenty-first-century pleasurable seaside urbanism, for the most part

The Palm Islands, Dubai, the largest palms in the world, as seen from space. The image is a composite of two scenes, acquired in 2008 by instruments on NASA's Terra satellite.

marketed to rich Westerners. But the shape of the largest palms in the world can only be appreciated fully from the air or from space.

Islands of Adventure and Abandon

The palm tree has also emerged as a key symbol in the visual representation of adventure islands, desert islands and tropical islands (and also desert oases – landlocked islands surrounded by sand rather than water). Fictional accounts of tropical islands often present them as separate bounded places surrounded by another often hostile or alien environment. Associated ideas include being stranded, shipwrecked and castaway; remoteness and isolation; a safe haven versus a realm of adventure and the quest for treasure; ways of escape; bringing civilization and order to the untamed natural world but also the possibility of nature as a source of danger and savagery; and the threat of newcomers, strangers and aliens, and the danger posed by pirates or savages.

From the early twentieth century this set of tensions has provided a rich vein for Western cartoonists to mine. Cartoons often portray a tiny desert island with just one or two palm trees and castaways pondering some irony interloping from the outside world.[21]

Yet some of the most famous desert island and adventure island fictions are surprisingly palm-light. The early standard-setting and much emulated island-centred adventure fiction was Daniel Defoe's *The Life and Strange Surprizing Adventures of Crusoe, of York, Mariner* (1719).[22] Defoe mentions a cabbage palm, 'something like the palmetto tree' and the 'abundance of cocoa trees', but this is not the palm-laden island so beloved of the subsequent book illustrators and film directors who sought to tropicalize the story by filling it with palms.

Similarly, Robert Louis Stevenson's *Treasure Island* (1883), the hugely influential children's story about islands and pirates, makes just one mention of a distant 'Palm Key'. Covered by 'many tall trees of the pine family', Treasure Island itself had 'grey, melancholy woods, and wild stone spires', leading the hero, Jim Hawkins, to bemoan that

HUSBAND (*wrecked on cannibal island*). "I know a bit of their lingo. They're going to fatten us up."
SLIM WIFE. "Oh, they couldn't be so cruel!"

Palms have become an essential element of the iconography of desert island cartoons.

'from the first look onward, I hated the very thought of Treasure Island.' It was not until Louis Rhead (1857–1926) got to work illustrating the 1915 edition of the book that palms began to make an appearance.

Much the same story is to be told of J. M. Barrie's *Peter Pan; or, the Boy Who Would Not Grow Up*, first produced as a stage play in 1904 and published as a novel, *Peter and Wendy*, in 1911. Although trees abound on the island of Neverland (Peter's underground home is reached through a hollow trunk) neither text mentions palms. Perhaps because of unexpected Neverland climate warming, four decades later the vegetative covering of the island had been transformed: palms proliferate in Disney's 1953 film animation.

The paradox of the three tales is that while tropical palms are absent from the texts, they are an essential element in the subsequent visual representations of the stories. Encouragingly for book illustrators and film-makers, other novels of the genre, such as *Der Schweizerische*

'I stood like one thunderstruck.' Palms were a necessary feature of *Robinson Crusoe* illustrations by the time this frontispiece appeared in a 1930s edition of the novel.

Robinson (The Swiss Family Robinson, 1812), *The Coral Island: A Tale of the Pacific Ocean* (1858) and *The Blue Lagoon* (1908), allocate a more central role to the plant.

The contemporary iconography of adventure islands demands palms. The plant is an unsurprising although key scene-setter in theme parks and movies exploiting the idea of tropical adventures. The world's theme-park capital, Orlando, Florida, makes much of the possibilities in both the long-established Adventureland, in the Walt Disney Corporation's Magic Kingdom, and the more-recent rival, Universal Studios' Islands of Adventure. Theme-park rides and their set dressings of palms have been exported around the world, with the iconic Pirates of the Caribbean ride, for example, migrating from its native U.S. habitat to settle in Paris, Tokyo and Shanghai. The ride has also spawned the commercially successful twenty-first-century *Pirates of the Caribbean* film series, the most recent in the palm-rich genre of swashbuckling pirate movies reaching back to *The Black Pirate* of 1926.

Within five years of the publication of *Treasure Island*, the landscape, people and palms of the Pacific's real tropical islands had entranced the story's author. In his posthumously published memoir, *In the South Seas*, Stevenson observes:

> The cocoa-palm, that giraffe of vegetables, so graceful, so ungainly, to the European eye so foreign, was to be seen crowding on the beach, and climbing and fringing the steep sides of mountains . . . It was longer ere we spied the native village, standing (in the universal fashion) close upon a curve of beach, close under a grove of palms; the sea in front growling and whitening on a concave arc of reef. For the cocoa-tree and the island man are both lovers and neighbours of the surf. 'The coral waxes, the palm grows, but man departs,' says the sad Tahitian proverb; but they are all three, so long as they endure, co-haunters of the beach.[23]

Today's travel and tourism industries use the palm as a standard visual signifier to denote tropical holidays, exotic and out-of-the-ordinary leisure and intensely desirable pleasure. This is a realm, or a dream, of sun, sea and sand, with palm trees used as a surrogate for some combination of passionate enjoyment and erotic fulfilment. The set of stereotypical images might include, for example, coconut palms on an empty sandy beach with gently lapping waves and a glorious sunset, or a hammock strung between two palms overlooking another pristine sandy beach but this time set against a backdrop of a brilliantly sunny sky and a crystal-clear blue sea. Such views are often empty of tourists; if they are included it won't be a crowd but instead perhaps one young woman sitting or lying on a palm stem that reclines gently out over the sea or a couple, hand-in-hand, strolling along the water's edge beside shady palm trees. Such generalized fantasy images pretend that tropical holidays are authentic, natural and exotic with endless possibilities for sensual enjoyment. In the process other holidaymakers are bypassed and the workers in the hotels and tourism industries, their families and wider society more generally are ignored. Similarly, the geography of real tropical coastlines, the artificiality of resort landscapes and the environmental impact of tourism are hidden behind the palm tree image.

One likely trophy from a holiday in, say, Saint Lucia or Bali is a short-sleeved tropical leisure shirt decorated with a palm motif. The garment that developed in Hawaii during the 1920s and '30s began life as a working shirt – sometimes made from kimono fabric brought to the archipelago by Japanese migrants – for sugar cane and pineapple plantation labourers.[24] After the Second World War the shirt, legitimized by American film stars and presidents, and like the coconut

Palm trees on tropical leisure shirts signifying the good life.
Castries Market, Saint Lucia, 2016.

palm centuries before, began a migration around the world's tropical coasts to become generic leisure apparel and signifier of a successful tropical holidaymaker.

Advertisers have also seized on the palm as an icon of desire, sensuality and eroticism to sell other things. The Bounty, a coconut and chocolate confectionary bar, exemplifies the genre. A 1954 magazine advertisement shows a young woman lying in a hammock and a coconut split open on a tropical beach fringed with palm fronds. The text states: 'NEW . . . far and away the most exotic chocolate treat. Bounty, with milkier, juicer coconut than even south-sea islanders ever knew.' By the 1990s TV commercials for the 'the taste of paradise', with their beaches and palms, had become romantically and sexually more explicit: eating a luscious Bounty bar was a good way to while away the time before a promising sexual encounter.

While advertisers may be limited in making palm eroticism too explicit, the experimental artist Sigmar Polke (1963–2010), fascinated by palms in various contexts, laid bare the associations between palm trees, tropical islands and sex in a pornographic 1973 print: it shows a cartoon castaway island occupied by naked women and a single man, while in the foreground another man gazes in amazement at the huge green priapic palm tree springing from his loins.[25]

Fiction writers have also sometimes used the priapic qualities of tall, erect palm trees, with their spurting verdant crowns, to convey and intensify imaginings of sexual abandon. The French writer Émile Zola (1840–1902) did this brilliantly in his 1871 novel *La Curée* (The Kill), using the device of a conservatory full of palms and other tropical plants as a setting and metaphor for the novel's two main characters' intense, uncontrollable and illicit lust for each other:

> The whole conservatory was in rut, the whole patch of virgin forest ablaze with the foliage and blossoms of the tropics.
>   Their senses warped, Maxime and Renée felt themselves caught up in the earth's powerful nuptials. Through the bearskin the ground burned their backs, and hot droplets

fell upon them from the tall palms. The sap rising in the trees' flanks penetrated them as well, filling them with wild desire for immediate increase, for reproduction on a gigantic scale. They partook of the conservatory's rut.[26]

A gentler interpretation of the theme of the palm's role in forbidden love, this time restrained and ultimately thwarted, is in the iconic British film *Brief Encounter* (1954). Noël Coward (1899–1973), author of the screenplay, uses the idea of the palm as alluring and seductive and yet something that, however reluctantly, must be rejected and resisted. As the film concludes, the heroine, Laura, recalls dozing on a train as she returns to her husband, dreaming of what might have been:

> I saw us leaning on the rail of a ship looking at the sea and stars – standing on some tropical beach in the moonlight with the palm trees sighing above us. Then the palm trees changed into those pollarded willows by the canal just before the level crossing and all the silly dreams disappeared and I got out at Ketchworth and gave up my ticket and walked home as usual – quite soberly and without wings – without any wings at all.[27]

The Palm and Destruction

Another vision of the palm-laden remote tropical island presents a potential haven twisted into a nightmare of savagery. In *Lord of the Flies* (1954) William Golding gives his palms a significant role in the process, using them to create mood and tension:

> A flurry of wind made the palms talk and the noise seemed very loud now that darkness and silence made it so noticeable. Two grey trunks rubbed each other with an evil speaking that no one had noticed by day.[28]

The theme of idyll turned malevolent also underlies Alex Garland's cult novel *The Beach* (1996), although palms play a minor part in his fiction. For the subsequent movie, however, the film-makers demanded that the beach used for filming met with their own and filmgoers' visual stereotype of a tropical beach paradise adorned with palms. Although providing a stunning coastal setting, the chosen location, Maya Bay, in the Phi Phi Islands off Thailand, was without the necessary iconic palms. The film-makers received official permission to temporarily remove the beach's indigenous vegetation, landscape the site and plant it with one hundred coconut palms that were to be removed and the beach restored when filming was complete. The proposals led to a barrage of protest and a legal battle over the environmental consequences of the project, which began before filming and continued long after the movie was released in 2000.

The paradox was that to meet Western visual expectations about the ideal tropical island in a film about a commune in a secret paradise, supposedly remote from modern society, the pristine and natural beach chosen for filming had to be transformed – by adding palm trees. The coconut palms became the 'symbolic icon' of the emergent protest.[29] In the event 73 palms were used. Despite post-filming restoration, the protestors argued that the damage to the beach was irreversible. The success of the film helped turn the beach, even without palms, into a significant tourist destination: it changed fundamentally. By 2016 there were 5,000 low-season visitors a day, with 'overcrowding an environmental disaster'.[30]

Palms have often provided the vegetative centre point for films portraying violence and malevolence on tropical shores. The most emblematic scenes, including the mesmerizing opening sequence, of *Apocalypse Now*, the epic American war film produced and co-written by Francis Ford Coppola and released in 1979, are of palm trees on the coast of Vietnam ablaze after being napalmed. A second, longer scene portrays the attack and destruction of a coastal village by American helicopters and soldiers. Lieutenant Colonel Bill Kilgore, the commander of the attack, which is being bogged down by mortars being

WHAT YOU MAKE CAN PREVENT THIS

The palm as a symbol of destruction: Second World War poster,
by artist Adolph Treidler.

fired from a palm grove, radios for assistance: 'Goddammit, I want
that tree line bombed! Bomb them into the Stone Age, son.' Minutes
later Phantom jets arrive, release their bombs and the palm grove
erupts into a conflagration, destroying the plants and the people hidden
den beneath them. Kilgore is delighted with the destruction, saying:

'You smell that? Do you smell that? Napalm, son – nothing else in the world smells like that. I love the smell of napalm in the morning.'[31]

The napalm scenes in *Apocalypse Now* were filmed in the Philippines and the palm grove was incinerated by igniting hundreds of gallons of gasoline poured over the plants.[32] And the 'palm' in the napalm used to destroy palms and people? Although the name remained the same, the napalm used in the Vietnam War contained different ingredients from the substance invented during the Second World War. The original napalm was developed in 1942 by Harvard University's Louis Fieser (1899–1977). The name was formed by combining letters from two of the ingredients: the first two of naphthenate with the first four of palmitate. The weapon stands apart from other incendiaries because it includes a gelling agent that sticks to whatever it touches and burns at an extremely high temperature.[33] The palmitate element helps provide the critical sticky gel. While palmitic acid, from which palmitate is derived, is in many natural substances, it was discovered in 1840 in saponified palm oil extracted from *palmitique* – the pith in palm stems – by French chemist Edmond Frémy (1814–1894), who was working on improving candles.

The film *Apocalypse Now* was awarded another palm, the Palme d'Or, at the Cannes Film Festival of 1979. The Palme d'Or, both the logo and the highest award of the annual festival (held adjacent to La Croisette, the palm-bedecked seafront boulevard), references the palm frond on the city's coat of arms, which, in turn, reflects the ancient use of the symbol by Lérins Abbey on a nearby Mediterranean island. The story goes that St Honoratus (*c.* 350–429), the founder of the abbey, prayed for the sea to cleanse the island of putrefaction and, as the prayer was answered, climbed a silver palm to escape the rising waters.[34]

As both Saint Honoratus' island miracle and the birth of Apollo on Delos illustrate, contemporary island fantasies featuring palm trees have precursors that reach back through millennia.

Timeline

100 million years ago	The oldest known palm fossils, dating from the Cretaceous Period, include leaves and stems
c. 56–34 million years ago	During the Eocene Epoch palms were abundant and widespread and included genera in existence today
c. 6,000 BCE	Archaeological remains show human use of dates, probably harvested from the wild
4,500–3,500 BCE	Domestication of the date palm (*Phoenix dactylifera*) in the Fertile Crescent
3000 BCE	A jar containing palm oil from West Africa is placed in a tomb at Abydos in Egypt as a burial good
c. 500 BCE	The date palm is introduced to southern Europe
c. 800 CE	The first coconuts, the drupe from *Cocos nucifera*, percolate into Europe
1460–82	Portuguese explorers travel to the coasts of West Africa and provide accounts of the oil palm (*Elaeis guineensis*) and the use of its oils by Africans
1490s	Date palms are planted in the New World shortly after the initial European journeys to the Americas

1499	Portuguese travellers journeying back to Europe introduce the Indian variety of coconut to the Cape Verde islands. From there it is distributed to other tropical Atlantic coasts
c. 1565	Spanish voyagers carry the coconut from the Philippines across the Pacific to South America
1568	The European fan palm (*Chamaerops humilis*) is planted in the world's first botanic garden at the University of Padua, Italy
1769	The first palms are planted in San Diego, California, by Father Serra
1780s	Casks of palm oil are auctioned in London
1818	The largest palm house in the world is designed by John Claudius Loudon and constructed for the London horticultural firm of Loddiges
1822	Completion of the remodelling of the Royal Pavilion, Brighton, by John Nash. Numerous palm motifs adorn the interior of the building, including cast-iron columns decorated as abstracted palm trees
1823	Publication of the first volume of Carl Friedrich Philipp von Martius's *Historia naturalis palmarum* (Natural History of Palms). The following year Martius publishes the first significant classificatory framework for palms
1848	Arrival of the oil palm in Southeast Asia: four plants are sent from Amsterdam to Java to be used ornamentally in the Buitenzorg botanic gardens. The Palm House opens at the Royal Botanic Gardens at Kew, West London
1849	The plant collector Robert Fortune sends specimens of the cold-tolerant Chusan palm (*Trachycarpus fortune*) from China to Britain. The species is subsequently planted successfully in many parts of Britain and other places with a temperate climate

1853	Publication of Alfred Russel Wallace's *Palm Trees of the Amazon and Their Uses*. While noting that fewer than 600 palm species were then known, Wallace believed that a more accurate figure would be 2,000
1856	Publication of *A Popular History of Palms and Their Allies* by Berthold Seemann
1864	The Canary Island date palm (*Phoenix canariensis*) is naturalized in Nice by Count Vigier and subsequently used to decorate many coastal boulevards of the Côte d'Azur
1884	Sunlight laundry soap, made with ingredients including palm oils, is produced by the British firm Lever Brothers. The Great Palm House opens in the botanic gardens in Dublin
1898	In the United States B. J. Johnson produces the first tablets of Palmolive toilet soap
1902	The invention of a chemical hydrogenation process allows the conversion of liquid vegetable oils (including palm kernel and coconut oils) into solid and semi-solid fats used in the production of margarine and by industrial bakeries
1909	William Lever plans the first oil palm plantations in the Belgian Congo
1917	The first commercial planting of the oil palm in Southeast Asia
1931	240 km (150 miles) of Los Angeles boulevards are planted with over 25,000 palm trees
1946–8	In some of his last paintings on canvas, Henri Matisse creates a series of still-life works featuring both the interior of his Côte d'Azur villa and the *Phoenix canariensis* dominating the view through his studio window
1957	Invention of instant noodles, using palm oil as a critical ingredient, in Japan

mid-1960s	West Africa maintains its long-established position as the dominant palm oil-producing region, with Nigeria responsible for over 40 per cent of global production
1967	David Hockney creates *A Bigger Splash*, a seminal painting of a swimming pool, modern house and palm trees, capturing a quintessential California day
1980–88	The prolonged armed conflict between Iran and Iraq destroys or severely damages many plantations in both countries' most important date-growing areas. Subsequent wider conflict continues to devastate date production in the region where the date was originally domesticated
2001	The Eden Project, 'the world's largest glasshouse', opens in Cornwall, southwest England; the Rainforest Biome housing palms and other tropical plants is 50 m (164 ft) high.Construction commences of the artificial Palm Islands off the coast of Dubai, UAE; Palm Jumeirah, the first island, is completed in 2014
2007	The discovery in Madagascar of *Tahina spectabilis*, the Tahina palm, remarkable as a 'suicide palm' that flowers once, after a period of between 35 to 50 years, and then dies; critically endangered, there are approximately thirty mature individual plants in the wild. Two years later, the Royal Botanic Gardens, Kew, announces the discovery of 24 new palm species, with twenty of them from Madagascar
2008	The second edition of *Genera Palmarum: The Evolution and Classification of Palms*, by John Dransfield and colleagues, provides a new classificatory framework for palms and details 183 palm genera
c. 2010	Insect attack and disease increasingly harms the ornamental Canary Island date palm in Europe and California. Lethal yellowing disease progressively devastates coconut palms in the Caribbean and Florida

2014	Palm oil production rises fiftyfold over the five decades from 1964 to over 61 million metric tons, with Indonesia and Malaysia producing 85 per cent of the world's supply. Palm oil now accounts for over 60 per cent of all vegetable oil traded internationally
2015	In the first nine months of the year, 100,000 fires are detected by satellite in Indonesia, the majority occurring in peatland areas to be used for oil palm plantations

References

𓆸

1 The Prince of Plants

1 Georg Kohlmaier and Barna von Sartory, *Houses of Glass: A Nineteenth-century Building Type* (Cambridge, MA, 1986), p. 49.

2 Dissecting the Giant Herb

1 Quoted in Religious Tract Society, *The Palm Tribes and their Varieties* (London, 1852), p. 100.
2 Global Biodiversity Information Facility, 'Latania lontaroides', www.gbif.org, accessed 3 January 2016.
3 Alfred Russel Wallace, *Palm Trees of the Amazon and Their Uses* (London, 1853), p. 1.
4 John Dransfield, Natalie W. Uhl, Conny B. Asmussen, William J. Baker, Madeline M. Harley and Carl E. Lewis, *Genera Palmarum: The Evolution and Classification of Palms* (London, 2008), pp. 131–9.
5 Ibid., pp. 91–103.
6 T. K. Broschat, M. L. Elliott and D. R. Hodel, 'Ornamental Palms: Biology and Horticulture', *Horticultural Reviews*, XLII, ed. Jules Janick (2014), pp. 1–120.
7 Dransfield et al., *Genera Palmarum*, p. 106.
8 Mark Riley Cardwell, 'Trees of the Amazon Rainforest – In Pictures', www.theguardian.com, 29 October 2013.
9 Dransfield et al., *Genera Palmarum*, p. 363.
10 Dennis V. Johnson, *Tropical Palms* (Rome, 1998).
11 Michael J. Balick, 'The Use of Palms by the Apinayé and Guajajara Indians of Northeastern Brazil', *Advances in Economic Biology*, VI (1988), pp. 65–90.
12 Richard Evan Schultes, 'Palms and Religion in the Northwest Amazon', *Príncipes*, XVIII/1 (1974), pp. 3–21.
13 Edward Balfour, *The Timber Trees, Timber and Fancy Woods, as also, the Forests of India and of Eastern and Southern Asia*, 3rd edn (Madras, 1870), p. 40.

203

3 The Civilizing Date

1 Daniel Zohary, Maria Hopf and Ehud Weiss, *Domestication of Plants in the Old World: The Origin and Spread of Domesticated Plants in Southwest Asia, Europe, and the Mediterranean Basin*, 4th edn (Oxford, 2012), p. 134.

2 Victor Hehn, *Cultivated Plants and Domesticated Animals in Their Migration from Asia to Europe* (Amsterdam, 1976), p. 202.

3 April Holloway, 'Extinct Tree Resurrected from Ancient Seeds is Now a Dad', www.ancient-origins.net, 29 March 2015.

4 Zohary et al., *Domestication of Plants*, pp. 131–2.

5 August Henry Pruessner, 'Date Culture in Ancient Babylonia', *American Journal of Semitic Languages and Literatures*, XXXVI/3 (1920), pp. 213–32.

6 Pruessner, 'Date Culture'; Joshua J. Mark, 'Ashurnasirpal II', www.ancient.eu, 9 July 2014.

7 Barbara Nevling Porter, 'Sacred Trees, Date Palms, and the Royal Persona of Ashurnasirpal II', *Journal of Near Eastern Studies*, LII/2 (1993), pp. 129–39.

8 Lloyd Weeks, 'Arabia', in *The Cambridge World Prehistory*, ed. Colin Renfrew and Paul Bahn (Cambridge, 2014), pp. 1596–616.

9 Irfan Shadîd, 'Pre-Islamic Arabia', in *The Cambridge History of Islam,* vol. 1A, ed. P. M. Holt et al. (Cambridge, 1977), pp. 3–29.

10 W. H. Barreveld, *Date Palm Products* (Rome, 1993).

11 Herodotus, *An Account of Egypt*, trans. G. C. Macaulay [1904] (ebook, 2006).

12 H. C. Hamilton and W. Falconer, 'Strabo, Geography', www.perseus.tufts.edu, accessed 1 June 2016.

13 'Date Palm', www.iranicaonline.org, accessed 8 December 2012.

14 Ibid.

15 Porter, 'Sacred Trees'; Mariana Giovino, *The Assyrian Sacred Tree: A History of Interpretations* (Göttingen, 2007); Lincoln Taiz and Lee Taiz, *Flora Unveiled: The Discovery and Denial of Sex in Plants* (New York, 2017), p. 222.

16 Nawal Nasrallah, *Dates: A Global History* (London, 2011).

17 Wafaa M. Amer, 'History of Botany Part 1: The Date Palm in Ancient History', www.levity.com, accessed 20 July 2014.

18 Quoted in Taiz and Taiz, *Flora Unveiled*, p. 279.

19 Edward William Lane, trans., *The Thousand and One Nights, Commonly Called, in England, the Arabian Nights' Entertainments* (London, 1839), p. 219.

20 Suleiman A. Mourad, 'Mary in the Qur'an: A Reexamination of her Presentation', in *The Qur'an in Its Historical Context*, ed. Gabriel Said Reynolds (Abingdon, 2008), pp. 167–73; Tom Holland, *In the Shadow of the Sword: The Battle for Global Empire and the End of the Ancient World* (London, 2012), pp. 48–9.

21 'Leto', www.theoi.com, accessed 24 November 2014.

22 'The Gospel of Pseudo-Matthew', at www.gnosis.org, accessed 24 November 2014.

23 Ibid.

24 Mourad, 'Mary in the Qur'an', p. 169.

25 Richard Cronin, 'Edward Lear and Tennyson's Nonsense', in *Tennyson Among the Poets: Bicentenary Essays*, ed. Robert Douglas-Fairhurst and Seamus Perry (Oxford, 2009), pp. 259–79.

26 'FAOSTAT: Crops', www.fao.org, accessed 17 December 2016; see also Muhammad Siddiq, Salah M. Aleid and Adel A. Kader, *Dates: Postharvest Science, Processing Technology and Health Benefits* (Chichester, 2014).

27 Shri Mohan Jain, Jameel M. Al-Khayri and Dennis V. Johnson, *Date Palm Biotechnology* (London, 2011); Layla Eplett, 'Save the Date: Preventing Heirloom Date Palm Extinction in Egypt's Siwa Oasis', www. scientificamerican.com, 17 November 2015.

28 'Date Palm', www.iranicaonline.org; Wassim Bessem, 'Iraqi Dates Shrivel Awaiting Production Means', www.al-monitor.com, 10 August 2015; Hannah Allam, 'War Uproots Iraq's Signature Date Palms, and Their Tenders', www.mcclatchydc.com, 23 June 2010.

4 Western Discovery

1 'Palm', www.etymonline.com, accessed 3 July 2012.

2 'Date', www.oed.com, accessed 4 July 2012.

3 Mary Clayton, *The Apocryphal Gospels of Mary in Anglo-Saxon England* (Cambridge, 1999).

4 M. Bradford Bedingfield, *The Dramatic Liturgy of Anglo-Saxon England* (Woodbridge, 2002), p. 107.

5 John Onians, *Bearers of Meaning: The Classical Orders in Antiquity, the Middle Ages, and the Renaissance* (Princeton, NJ, 1988), p. 76; Charles B. McClendon, *The Origins of Medieval Architecture: Building in Europe, AD 600–900* (New Haven, CT, 2005), pp. 132–6.

6 D. Rivera et al., 'Historical Evidence of the Spanish Introduction of Date Palm (*Phoenix dactylifera* L., Arecaceae) into the Americas', *Genetic Resources and Crop Evolution*, LX (2013), pp. 1433–52.

7 Emily Aleev-Snow, 'Exploring Coconut Migration Patterns: A Falcon-shaped Standing Cup', www.unmakingthings.rca.ac.uk, accessed 1 January 2016.

8 Michael Graves-Johnston, 'Early Africa Travel Literature', www.ilab.org, 22 June 2011.

9 Rivera et al., 'Historical Evidence of the Spanish Introduction of Date Palm'.

10 Heidi Trent and Joey Seymour, 'Examining California's First Palm Tree: The Serra Palm', *Journal of San Diego History*, LVI/3 (2010), pp. 105–20.

11 Gonzalo Fernández de Oviedo, *Natural History of the West Indies*, ed. and trans. Sterling A. Stroudemire (Chapel Hill, NC, 1959), p. 83.

12 Antonio Pigafetta, *Magellan's Voyage Around the World*, trans. James Alexander Robertson (Cleveland, OH, 1906), p. 101.

13 G. Hartwig, *The Polar and Tropical Worlds: A Description of Man and Nature in the Polar and Equatorial Regions of the Globe* (Philadelphia, PA, 1871), p. 539.

14 Bee F. Gunn, Luc Baudouin and Kenneth M. Olsen, 'Independent Origins of Cultivated Coconut (*Cocos nucifera* L.) in the Old World Tropics', www.journals.plos.org, 22 June 2011.

15 Charles R. Clement et al., 'Coconuts in the Americas', *Botanical Review*, LXXIX/3 (2013), pp. 342–70.

16 'The Voyage and Trauell of M. Cæsar Fredericke, Marchant of Venice, into the East India, and beyond the Indies', in *The Principal Navigations, Voyages, Traffiques and Discoveries of the English Nation*, vol. IX, coll. Richard Hakluyt, ed. Edmund Goldsmid, ebook (Adelaide, 2014).

17 Ibid.

18 Jean Barbot, *A Description of the Coasts of North and South-Guinea: And of the Ethiopia Inferior, Vulgarly Angola: Being a New and Accurate Account of the Western Maritime Countries of Africa . . .* (London, 1732), p. 202.

19 Ibid.

20 Ibid.

21 Sir Charles Lawson, *Memories of Madras* (London, 1905), p. 240.

22 Ali Foad Toulba, *Ceylon, the Land of Eternal Charm* (London, 1926), p. 135.

23 Robert Kerr, *A General History and Collection of Voyages and Travels, Arranged in Systematic Order: Forming a Complete History of the Origin and Progress of Navigation, Discovery, and Commerce, by Sea and Land, from the Earliest Ages to the Present Time* (Edinburgh, 1824). vol. II, pp. 230–31.

24 Sir Joseph Banks, *The Endeavour Journal of Sir Joseph Banks*, www.gutenberg. net.au, accessed 10 July 2015.

25 Ian E. Henson, 'A Brief History of the Oil Palm', in *Palm Oil: Production, Processing, Characterization, and Uses*, ed. Oi-Ming Lai et al. (Urbana, IL, 2012), pp. 1–30.

26 R.H.V. Corley and P.B.H. Tinker, *The Oil Palm* (London, 2008).

27 Martin Lynn, *Commerce and Economic Change in West Africa: The Palm Oil Trade in the Nineteenth Century* (Cambridge, 1997), p. 1.

28 Barbot, *A Description of the Coasts of North and South-Guinea*, p. 204.

29 Hans Sloane, *A Voyage to the Islands Madera, Barbados, Nieves, S. Christophers and Jamaica, with the Natural History of . . . the Last of Those Islands* (London, 1725), vol. II, p. 114.

30 John Adams, *Remarks on the Country Extending from Cape Palmas to the River Congo: Including Observations on the Manners and Customs of the Inhabitants* (London, 1823), pp. 171–2.

31 Griffith Hughes, *The Natural History of Barbados* (London, 1750), p. 112.

32 Sloane, *A Voyage*, p. 114.

33 *The Times*, 30 December 1800.

5 Empire and Utility

1 Quoted in C. R. Fay, *Palace of Industry, 1851: A Study of the Great Exhibition and Its Fruits* (Cambridge, 1951), p. 47.

2 Robert Ellis, *Official Descriptive and Illustrated Catalogue of the Great Exhibition of the Works of Industry of All Nations, 1851* (London, 1851), vol. III, p. 687.

3 Religious Tract Society, *The Palm Tribes and Their Varieties* (London, 1852), p. 190.
4 Sophy Moody, *The Palm Tree* (London, 1864), p. xiii.
5 Edward Forbes, 'On the Vegetable World as Contributing to the Great Exhibition', in *The Art Journal Illustrated Catalogue: The Industry of All Nations* (London, 1851), pp. i–viii, quote p. iii.
6 Ibid., pp. iv–v.
7 J. G. Strutt, ed., *Tallis's History and Description of the Crystal Palace and the Exhibition of the World's Industry in 1851* (London, 1852), p. 133.
8 Thomas Treloar, *The Prince of Palms: Being a Short Account of the Cocoa-nut Tree, Showing the Uses to Which the Various Parts are Applied, Both by the Natives of India and Europeans* (London, 1852), p. 3.
9 Hugh C. Harries, 'Fun Made the Fair Coconut Shy', *Palms*, XLVIII/2 (2004), pp. 77–82.
10 Strutt, *Tallis's History*, p. 176.
11 Ibid.
12 John Adams, *Remarks on the Country Extending from Cape Palmas to the River Congo: Including Observations on the Manners and Customs of the Inhabitants* (London, 1823), p. 143.
13 Allan McPhee, *The Economic Revolution in British West Africa* (London, 1926), p. 25.
14 Ibid., p. 35.
15 Martin Lynn, *Commerce and Economic Change in West Africa: The Palm Oil Trade in the Nineteenth Century* (Cambridge, 1997), pp. 39–59.
16 Ibid., p. 3.
17 Ibid., p. 66.
18 Ibid., p. 89.
19 Stephanie Newell, 'Dirty Whites: "Ruffian-writing" in Colonial West Africa', *Research in African Literatures*, XXXIX/4 (2008), pp. 1–13.
20 *The Times*, 2 April 1798.
21 *The Times*, 20 November 1828.
22 Lynn, *Commerce and Economic Change*, p. 124.
23 Quoted in Alan Pim, *The Financial and Economic History of the African Tropical Territories* (Oxford, 1940), p. 39.
24 Lynn, *Commerce and Economic Change*.
25 Charles Wilson, *The History of Unilever* (London, 1954), vol. I, p. 31.
26 Colin Bell and Rose Bell, *City Fathers: The Early History of Town Planning in Britain* (Harmondsworth, 1972), p. 285.
27 Adam Macqueen, *The King of Sunlight: How William Lever Cleaned up the World* (London, 2004), p. 74.
28 Gillian Darley, *Villages of Vision* (London, 1978), pp. 140–44.
29 Lynn, *Commerce and Economic Change*, p. 3.
30 Anne McClintock, *Imperial Leather: Race, Gender and Sexuality in the Colonial Context* (London, 1995).
31 See Adam Hochschild, *King Leopold's Ghost: A Story of Greed, Terror and Heroism in Colonial Africa* (London, 1998); and Aldwin Roes (2010) 'Towards a

History of Mass Violence in the Etat Indépendant du Congo, 1885–1908', *South African Historical Journal*, LXII/4 (2010), pp. 634–70.

32 Wilson, *The History of Unilever*, vol. I, p. 179.

33 Quoted in William Hulme Lever, *Viscount Leverhulme: By His Son* (London, 1927), p. 173.

34 Ibid., p. 172.

35 Charles Wilson, *The History of Unilever*, vol. II, p. 324.

36 Macqueen, *The King of Sunlight*, p. 205.

37 Jules Marchal, *Lord Leverhulme's Ghosts: Colonial Exploitation in the Congo* (London, 2008).

38 Philip Ward-Jackson, *Public Sculpture of the City of London* (Liverpool, 2003), p. 281. See also Phillip Medhurst, 'Walter Gilbert Main Inventory', www.scribd.com, 10 July 2009.

39 Todd Kuchta, *Semi-detached Empire: Suburbia and the Colonization of Britain, 1880 to the Present* (Charlottesville, VA, 2010), pp. 111–12.

40 K. G. Berger and S. M. Martin, 'Palm Oil', in *The Cambridge World History of Food*, vol. I, ed. Kenneth F. Kiple and Kriemhild Coneè Ornelas (Cambridge, 2000), pp. 397–410.

41 Pim, *Financial and Economic History*, quote p. 88.

42 Ibid., quote p. 75.

6 Of Tigers, Plantations and Instant Noodles

1 Hillary Rosner, 'Palm Oil is Everywhere: This is What to Do About it', www.ensia.com, 30 October 2013.

2 'World: World Palm Oil, 1964–2013', www.agrimoney.com, 12 May 2015; 'Oilseeds: World Markets and Trade', www.fas.usda.gov, 9 July 2015. Unless otherwise stated the figures in this chapter come from the Foreign Agricultural Service of the United States Department of Agriculture and concern palm oil alone (and not palm kernel oil).

3 Georgia Woodroffe, 'Palm Oil: A Slippery Issue', www.nouse.co.uk, 22 December 2014.

4 Rhett A. Butler, 'How Does the Global Commodity Collapse Impact Forest Conservation?', www.news.mongabay.com, 21 December 2015.

5 Ursula Biermann et al., 'Oils and Fats as Renewable Raw Materials in Chemistry', *Angewandte Chemie International Edition*, L/17 (2011), pp. 3854–71.

6 Wilmar International Limited, 'Corporate Profile', www.wilmar-international.com, accessed 12 January 2016.

7 'Singapore Developer behind London's Latest Skyscraper', www.property-report.com, 9 December 2015.

8 Greenpeace India, *Frying the Forest: How India's use of Palm Oil is Having a Devastating Impact on Indonesia's Rainforests, Tigers and the Global Climate* (Bengaluru, 2012).

9 WWF, *Palm Oil Buyers Scorecard: Measuring the Progress of Palm Oil Buyers* (Gland, 2013), p. 56; World Instant Noodles Association, www.instantnoodles.org, accessed 9 November 2015.

10 Noah Kaufman, 'Instant Ramen is Japan's Greatest Invention Says Japan', www.foodandwine.com, 6 July 2015.

11 Osaka Convention and Tourism Bureau, 'Let's Go to the Instant Ramen Museum!', www.osaka-info.jp, accessed 9 November 2015.

12 Shoot Kian Yeong, Zainab Idris and Hazimah Abu Hassan, 'Palm Oleochemicals in Non-food Applications', in *Palm Oil: Production, Processing, Characterization, and Uses*, ed. Oi-Ming Lai et al. (Urbana, IL, 2012), pp. 587–624.

13 Wilmar International Limited, *Part of Your life: Specialty Fats Products* (Singapore, 2011), p. 9.

14 Oliver Pye and Jayati Bhattacharya, eds, *The Palm Oil Controversy in Southeast Asia: A Transnational Perspective* (Singapore, 2013).

15 Greenpeace, *Licence to Kill: How Deforestation for Palm Oil is Driving Sumatran Tigers Towards Extinction* (Amsterdam, 2013).

16 Erik Meijaard, 'Football Fields of Deforestation: But What Does That Mean?', www.tropicalbiology.org, 18 December 2014.

17 Greenpeace, *Licence to Kill*, p. 23.

18 Union of Concerned Scientists, 'Palm Oil and Global Warming', www.ucsusa.org, accessed 23 September 2015.

19 Nancy Harris, Susan Minnemeyer, Fred Stolle and Octavia Aris Payne, 'Indonesia's Fire Outbreaks Producing More Daily Emissions than Entire U.S. Economy', www.wri.org, 16 October 2015.

20 Rhett A. Butler, 'Plantation Companies Challenged by Haze-causing Fires in Indonesia', www.news.mongabay.com, 14 October 2015; Lindsey Allen, 'Is Indonesia's Fire Crisis Connected to the Palm Oil in Our Snack Food?', www.theguardian.com, 23 October 2015; Greenpeace, *Indonesia's Forests: Under Fire: Indonesia's Fire Crisis is a Test of Corporate Commitment to Forest Protection* (Amsterdam, 2015).

21 Sara Jerving, '"We Want Our Land Back": Liberian Communities Speak Out About Big Palm Oil', www.news.mongabay.com, 10 August 2015.

22 Pieter J. H. van Beukering, Herman S. J. Cesar and Marco A. Janssen, 'Economic valuation of the Leuser National Park on Sumatra, Indonesia', *Ecological Economics*, XLIV/1 (2003), pp. 43–62, quote p. 61.

23 Sara Jerving, 'Will Palm Oil Help Liberia? Industry Expansion Has Critics Crying Foul', www.news.mongabay.com, 11 August 2015.

24 GRAIN and RIAO-RDC, 'Agro-colonialism in the Congo: European and U.S. Development Finance Bankrolls a New Round of Agro-colonialism in the DRC', www.grain.org, 2 June 2015.

25 EFSA Panel on Contaminants in the Food Chain, 'Scientific Opinion on the Risks for Human Health Related to the Presence of 3- and 2-monochloropropanediol (MCPD), and Their Fatty Acid Esters, and Glycidyl Fatty Acid Esters in Food', EFSA *Journal*, XIV/5 (2016); Ben Chapman, 'Nutella Maker Fights Back Against Fears Over Cancer-causing Palm Oil', www.independent.co.uk, 11 January 2017.

26 'Alternative Names for Palm', www.palmoilinvestigations.org, accessed 13 November 2015.

27　WWF, 'Which Everyday Products Contain Palm Oil?', www.worldwildlife.
org, accessed 23 September 2015.

28　Marion O'Leary, 'Palm Free Shampoo?', www.mokosh.com.au,
17 September 2013.

29　Greenpeace, *Licence to Kill*; Rainforest Action Network, *Testing
Commitments to Cut Conflict Palm Oil* (San Francisco, CA, 2015);
www.palmoilinvestigations.org; WWF, *Palm Oil Buyers Scorecard*; Union
of Concerned Scientists, 'Palm Oil and Global Warming'.

30　Hanna Thomas, 'Starbucks and Palm Oil, Wake Up and Smell the Coffee',
www.theguardian.com, 25 August 2015; Greenpeace, *Licence to Kill*.

31　Sime Darby Plantation, *Sustainability Report 2014* (Selangor Darul Ehsan,
2014); Wilmar International Ltd, *Annual Report 2014* (Singapore, 2015);
European Palm Oil Alliance, 'The Palm Oil Story, Facts and Figures',
www. palmoilandfood.eu, accessed 5 August 2015; Palm Oil World,
'Official Palm Oil Information Source', www.palmoilworld.org, accessed
13 November 2015; Sime Darby, 'Palm Oil Facts and Figures',
www.simedarby.com, accessed 5 August 2015.

32　Union of Concerned Scientists, *Fries, Face Wash, Forests: Scoring America's Top
Brands on Their Palm Oil Commitments* (Cambridge, MA, 2015).

33　Roundtable on Sustainable Palm Oil, 'About Us', www.rspo.org, accessed
5 November 2015.

34　Roundtable on Sustainable Palm Oil, *Impact Update 2015* (Kuala Lumpur,
2015).

35　Sustainable Palm Oil Platform, 'Roundtable on Sustainable Palm Oil
(RSPO)', www.sustainablepalmoil.org, accessed 5 November 2015.

36　Nils Klawitter, 'A Tangle of Conflicts: The Dirty Business of Palm Oil',
www.spiegel.de, 2 May 2014.

37　Unilever, 'Transforming the Palm Oil Industry', www.unilever.com,
accessed 26 January 2016; Colgate-Palmolive Company, *Colgate
Sustainability Report 2014: Giving the World Reasons to Smile* (New York, 2015).

38　Unilever, *Making Sustainable Living Commonplace: Annual Report and Accounts 2015:
Strategic Report* (Rotterdam and London, 2015), p. 24.

39　Greenpeace, *Cutting Deforestation Out of the Palm Oil Supply Chain: Company
Scorecard* (Amsterdam, 2016).

40　Rebecca Campbell, 'How Green Are Vegetable and Rapeseed Oils?',
www.theecologist.org, 12 May 2012.

7 The Ornamental Palm

1　'The History of Botanic Gardens', www.bgci.org, accessed 2 March 2016.

2　'Sir Seewoosagur Ramgoolam Botanical Garden', www.lonelyplanet.com,
accessed 1 March 2016.

3　Shakunt Pandey, '225 Years of British History', www.nopr.niscair.res.in,
June 2012.

4　'Royal Botanical Gardens, Peradeniya', www.botanicgardens.gov.lk,
accessed 1 March 2016.

5 'History', www. en.jbrj.gov.br, accessed 1 May 2016.

6 Antonella Miola, 'The Botanical Garden of Padua University', www.coimbra-group.eu, accessed 10 April 2016.

7 Fred Gray, *Designing the Seaside: Architecture, Society and Nature* (London, 2006).

8 Michel Racine, Ernest J. P. Boursier-Mougenot and Françoise Binet, *The Gardens of Provence and the French Riviera* (Cambridge, MA, 1987); Philippe Collas and Éric Villedary, *Edith Wharton's French Riviera* (Paris, 2002), p. 31.

9 Orvar Löfgren, *On Holiday: A History of Vacationing* (Berkeley, CA, 1999), p. 219.

10 Robert L. Wiegel, 'Waikiki Beach, Oahu, Hawaii: History of Its transformation from a Natural to an Urban Shore', *Shore and Beach*, LXXVI/2 (2008), pp. 3–30; 'History of the Land', www.historichawaii.org, accessed 1 May 2016.

11 J. Smeaton Chase, *Our Araby: Palm Springs and the Garden of the Sun* (Palm Springs, CA, 1920), p. 28.

12 Jared Farmer, *Trees in Paradise: A California History* (New York, 2013), p. 342.

13 Richard A. Marconi and Debi Murray, *Images of America: Palm Beach* (San Francisco, CA, 2009).

14 'Winter Holidays in Palm Beach', *The Lotus Magazine*, VII (1916), pp. 181–2.

15 Farmer, *Trees in Paradise*; Victoria Dailey, 'Piety and Perversity: The Palms of Los Angeles', www.lareviewofbooks.org, 14 July 2014.

16 Nathan Masters, 'A Brief History of Palm Trees in Southern California', www.kcet.org, 7 December 2011.

17 Nathan Masters, 'CityDig: L.A.'s Oldest Palm Tree', www.lamab.com, 17 April 2013.

18 Nancy E. Loe, *Hearst Castle: An Interpretive History of W. R. Hearst's San Simeon Estate* (Santa Barbara, CA, 1994), pp. 38–9.

19 Kathy Arnold, 'Down on the Palm Farm', www.telegraph.co.uk, 16 April 2002.

20 See www.palmsandtrees.com, accessed 10 April 2016.

21 Farmer, *Trees in Paradise*, p. 412.

22 Will Coldwell, '10 of the Best Urban Beaches and City Riversides in Europe', www.theguardian.com, 11 July 2016.

23 Mike Nelhams, *Tresco Abbey Gardens: The Garden Guide* (Truro, 2008).

24 'Where the Fal meets the Med', www.westbriton.co.uk, 18 July 2009.

25 Tim Smit, *The Lost Gardens of Heligan* (London, 1997), p. 136.

26 Mark Brent, 'Palms', in *Gardening on the Edge: Drawing on the Cornwall Experience*, ed. Philip McMillan Browse (Penzance, 2004), pp. 87–110.

27 Smit, *The Lost Gardens*; 'Timeline', www.heligan.com, accessed 2 February 2016.

28 Margaret Bream, 'Wild in the City: Why the Riviera's Palms are Dying', www.thestar.com, 30 May 2015.

29 'Dying Off: Antigua's Struggle to Save the Coconut Palm', www.antiguaobserver.com, 28 December 2015.

30 E. Eziashi and I. Omamor, 'Lethal Yellowing Disease of the Coconut Palms (*Cocos nucifera l.*): An Overview of the Crises', *African Journal of Biotechnology*, IX/54 (2010), pp. 9122–7, quote p. 9125.

31 Centre for Agriculture and Bioscience International, 'Candidatus Phytoplasma palmae (lethal yellowing of coconut)', www.cabi.org, 20 January 2015.

32 Jerry Wilkinson, 'The Florida Keys Memorial', www.keyshistory.org, accessed 10 July 2015.

8 Captive Performer

1 J. C. Loudon, *Remarks on the Construction of Hothouses: Also, a Review of the Various Methods of Building Them in Foreign Countries as Well as in England* (London, 1817), p. 49.

2 William Jackson Hooker, *Botanical Miscellany* (London, 1830), pp. 74–5.

3 David Solman, *Loddiges of Hackney: The Largest Hothouse in the World* (London, 1995), p. 36.

4 G. F. Chadwick, 'Paxton and the Great Stove', *Architectural History*, IV (1961), pp. 77–92; Stefan Koppelkamm, *Glasshouses and Wintergardens of the Nineteenth Century* (St Albans, 1982), pp. 22–4.

5 'Palm House and Rose Garden', www.kew.org, accessed 1 May 2016.

6 Sue Minter, *The Greatest Glasshouse: The Rainforests Recreated* (London, 1990).

7 Paula Deitz, *Of Gardens: Selected Essays* (Philadelphia, PA, 2011), p. 108.

8 'Removal of a Gigantic Palm-tree', *Illustrated London News*, 4 August 1854.

9 Samuel Phillips, *Guide to the Crystal Palace and Park* (London, 1854), p. 64.

10 Samuel Phillips and F. K. J. Shenton, *Official General Guide to the Crystal Palace and Park* (London, 1858), p. 126.

11 *The Times*, 20 January 1855.

12 Quoted in J. R. Piggott, *Palace of the People: The Crystal Palace at Sydenham 1854–1936* (London, 2004), p. 172.

13 Eileen McCracken, *The Palm House and Botanic Garden, Belfast* (Belfast, 1971).

14 'Restoration of the Curvilinear Range of the National Botanic Gardens, Glasnevin, Dublin', www.bgci.org, June 1996.

15 'Dublin Palm House Wins EU Heritage Award', www.bgci.org, 17 March 2006.

16 Georg Kohlmaier and Barna von Sartory, *Houses of Glass: A Nineteenth-century Building Type* (Cambridge, MA, 1986), quote p. 241.

17 Colin G. Calloway, Gerd Gemunden and Susanne Zantop, eds, *Germans and Indians: Fantasies, Encounters, Projections* (Lincoln, NE, 2002), p. 71.

18 'Residence Museum: Conservatories of Max II and Ludwigs II – Exhibition', www.residenz-muenchen.de, accessed 1 May 2016.

19 K. G. Tkachenko, '"Peter the Great" Botanical Garden Celebrates 300 Years', www.agrowebcee.net, accessed 10 April 2016; 'The Saint-Petersburg University Botanic Garden', www.coimbra-group.eu, accessed 10 April 2016.

20 Harold R. Fletcher and William H. Brown, *The Royal Botanic Garden Edinburgh 1670–1970* (Edinburgh, 1970), p. 143.
21 Ibid., pp. 174–5.
22 Osbert Lancaster, *All Done from Memory* (London, 1963), pp. 58–60.
23 Deitz, *Of Gardens*; Minter, *The Greatest Glasshouse*.
24 Koppelkamm, *Glasshouses and Wintergardens*, p. 106; 'Enid A. Haupt Conservatory', www.nybg.org, accessed 2 May 2016.
25 'Dublin Palm House', www.bgci.org, accessed 2 May 2016.
26 Glenn Collins, 'Palms Return to an Island (Manhattan): A Major Replanting as the Winter Garden Prepares to Reopen', www.nytimes. com, 13 August 2002; Julie Shapiro, 'Replacement Palm Trees Planted in Battery Park City's Winter Garden, www.dnainfo.com, 20 August 2013.
27 'Tropical Rainforest', www.espacepourlavie.ca, accessed 10 April 2016; 'Montréal Biodôme', www.thecanadianencyclopedia.ca, accessed 10 April 2016.
28 'The Largest Greenhouse in the World', www.twistedsifter.com, 13 September 2012.
29 'Rosemont Five Star Hotel and Residences', www.zasa.com, accessed 1 July 2016.
30 Kim Megson, 'Skyscraping Rainforest to Be Centrepiece of Under-development Dubai Rosemont', www.attractionsmanagement.com, 27 July 2016.
31 Oliver Smith, 'New Dubai Hotel to Feature its Own Rainforest and Aquarium', www.thetelegraph.co.uk, 15 August 2016.

9 Abstractions and Fantasies

1 Margaret Ashton, *Broken Idols of the English Reformation* (Cambridge, 2015), p. 325.
2 Anna Keay, *The Magnificent Monarch: Charles II and the Ceremonies of Power* (London, 2008), pp. 98–9.
3 Gauvin Alexander Bailey, *The Spiritual Rococo: Decor and Divinity from the Salons of Paris to the Missions of Patagonia* (Farnham, 2014), p. 97.
4 Alexandra Loske, personal communication, 20 November 2012.
5 'Palm Room', www.spencerhouse.co.uk, accessed 16 August 2016.
6 'Bayreuth New Palace: Margrave's Rooms: Palm Room', www.bayreuth-wilhelmine.de, accessed 12 August 2016.
7 Dorinda Outram, *Panorama of the Enlightenment* (Los Angeles, CA, 2006), p. 234; Patrick Conner, *Oriental Architecture in the West* (London, 1979), pp. 24–5.
8 John Nash, *Views of the Royal Pavilion* (London, 1991).
9 Raymond Lister, *Decorative Cast Ironwork in Great Britain* (London, 1960), p. 152.
10 David Watkin, 'The Migration of the Palm: A Case-study of Architectural Ornament as a Vehicle of Meaning', *Apollo*, CXXXII (1990), pp. 78–84, quote p. 79.

11 E. Graeme Robertson and Joan Robertson, *Cast Iron Decoration: A World Survey* (London, 1977).

12 Jared Farmer, *Trees in Paradise: A California History* (New York, 2013), p. 337.

13 Ibid.; Sean Brawley and Chris Dixon, *The South Seas: A Reception History from Daniel Defoe to Dorothy Lamour* (Lanham, MD, 2015).

14 Flavia Frigeri, 'How Matisse Was Seduced by the Palm Tree', www.tate. org.uk, 22 August 2014.

15 Fred Gray, *Designing the Seaside: Architecture, Society and Nature* (London, 2006), pp. 106–14.

16 'Preserved Palm Trees', www.preservedpalm.net, accessed 12 August 2016.

17 Dolly Jørgensen, 'The Palm Islands, Dubai, UAE', in *Iconic Designs: 50 Stories about 50 Things*, ed. Grace Lees-Maffei (London, 2014), pp. 62–6.

18 Yasser Elsheshtawy, *Dubai: Behind an Urban Spectacle* (Abingdon, 2010), quote p. 143.

19 Christian Steiner, 'Iconic Spaces, Symbolic Capital and the Political Economy of Urban Development in the Arab Gulf', in *Under Construction: Logics of Urbanism in the Gulf Region*, ed. Steffen Wippel et al. (London, 2016), pp. 17–30.

20 Ibid., p. 26.

21 Bruce Handy, 'A Guy, a Palm Tree, and a Desert Island: The Cartoon Genre that Just Won't Die', www.vanityfair.com, 25 May 2012.

22 Deborah Philips, *Fairground Attractions: A Genealogy of the Pleasure Ground* (London 2012), chap. 8.

23 Robert Louis Stevenson, *In the South Seas* (New York, 1907), p. 4.

24 DeSoto Brown and Linda Arthur, *The Art of the Ahola Shirt* (Waipahu, HI, 2008).

25 'Jill Krementz Covers Sigmar Polke at MOMA', www.newyorksocialdiary. com, 25 April 2015.

26 Émile Zola, *The Kill*, trans. Arthur Goldhammer (New York, 2005), p. 176.

27 Noël Coward, *Noël Coward Screenplays: In Which We Serve, Brief Encounter, The Astonished Heart* (London, 2015), pp. 307–8.

28 William Golding, *Lord of the Flies*, paperback edn (London, 2005), p. 91.

29 Erik Cohen, *Explorations in Thai Tourism: Collected Case Studies* (Bingley, 2008), p. 60.

30 Terry Fredrickson, 'Phi Phi's Maya Bay: Overcrowding an Environmental Disaster', www.bangkokpost.com, 7 July 2016.

31 John Milius and Francis Ford Coppola, *Apocalypse Now Redux: An Original Screenplay*, www.dailyscript.com, accessed 1 July 2013.

32 Kevin Forde, 'The 5 Most Horrifyingly Wasteful Film Shoots', www.cracked.com, 14 December 2011.

33 Robert M. Neer, *Napalm: An American Biography* (Cambridge, MA, 2013).

34 'Discover Cannes Guidebook', www.cannes-destination.com, accessed 1 July 2014.

Further Reading

꒐

There is a vast contemporary literature about the palm. It extends, for example, from dozens of books lauding the nutritional benefits of coconut oil through to detailed manuals about the science and commercial exploitation of the date palm and oil palm. The books listed here include some accessible case studies of particular topics, nineteenth-century palm classics and present-day reports presenting different dimensions of the bitter palm oil controversy.

Dransfield, John, Natalie W. Uhl, Conny B. Asmussen, William J. Baker, Madeline M. Harley and Carl E. Lewis, *Genera Palmarum: The Evolution and Classification of Palms* (London, 2008)
Farmer, Jared, *Trees in Paradise: A California History* (New York, 2013)
Greenpeace, *Licence to Kill: How Deforestation for Palm Oil is Driving Sumatran Tigers Toward Extinction* (Amsterdam, 2013)
—, *Cutting Deforestation Out of the Palm Oil Supply Chain: Company Scorecard* (Amsterdam, 2016)
Greenpeace India, *Frying the Forest: How India's use of Palm Oil is having a Devastating Impact on Indonesia's Rainforests, Tigers and the Global Climate* (Bengaluru, 2012)
Kohlmaier, Georg, and Barna von Sartory, *Houses of Glass: A Nineteenth-century Building Type* (Cambridge, MA, 1986)
Koppelkamm, Stefan, *Glasshouses and Wintergardens of the Nineteenth Century* (St Albans, 1981)
Lack, Walter H., and Petra Lamers-Schutze, *Martius: The Book of Palms* (Cologne, 2010)
Lynn, Martin, *Commerce and Economic Change in West Africa: The Palm Oil Trade in the Nineteenth Century* (Cambridge, 1997)
Moody, Sophy, *The Palm Tree* (London, 1864)
Pye, Oliver, and Jayati Bhattacharya, eds, *The Palm Oil Controversy in Southeast Asia: A Transnational Perspective* (Singapore, 2013)
Rainforest Action Network, *Testing Commitments to Cut Conflict Palm Oil* (San Francisco, CA, 2015)
Religious Tract Society, *The Palm Tribes and Their Varieties* (London, 1852)

Riffle, Robert Lee, Paul Craft and Scott Zona, *The Encyclopedia of Cultivated Palms* (Portland, OR, 2012)

Roundtable on Sustainable Palm Oil, *Impact Update 2016* (Kuala Lumpur, 2016)

Union of Concerned Scientists, *Fries, Face Wash, Forests: Scoring America's Top Brands on Their Palm Oil Commitments* (Cambridge, MA, 2015)

Wallace, Alfred Russel, *Palm Trees of the Amazon and Their Uses* (London, 1853)

WWF, *Palm Oil Buyers Scorecard: Measuring the Progress of Palm Oil Buyers* (Gland, 2016)

Associations and Websites

BOTANIC GARDENS CONSERVATION INTERNATIONAL
An organization representing five hundred botanic gardens
in over one hundred countries
www.bgci.org

EUROPEAN PALM OIL ALLIANCE (EPOA)
Funded by global companies that produce, process and use palm oil,
EPOA seeks to 'rebalance the debate on palm oil and food'
www.palmoilandfood.eu

FAIRCHILD TROPICAL BOTANIC GARDEN
A botanic garden in Coral Gables, Florida, featuring a large
collection of palms in the Montgomery Palmetum.
www.fairchildgarden.org

GREENPEACE INTERNATIONAL
A non-governmental environmental organization exposing and challenging
the negative human and environmental consequences of palm oil
www.greenpeace.org

INTERNATIONAL PALM SOCIETY (IPS)
A long-established American society, with many international affiliate
organizations, providing a comprehensive source of information on palms,
designed particularly for amateur palm growers and palm enthusiasts
www.palms.org

PALM AND CYCAD SOCIETIES OF AUSTRALIA, EUROPEAN PALM SOCIETY
AND ASSOCIATION FOUS DE PALMIERS
The Australian, European and French varieties of the IPS
www.pacsoa.org.au
www.palmsociety.org.uk
www.fousdepalmiers.com

PALM OIL INVESTIGATIONS (POI)
Established in 2013, POI is the world's largest
palm oil consumer activist movement
www.palmoilinvestigations.org

PALMPEDIA
A photograph-rich website run for and by palm devotees
www.palmpedia.net

PALMWEB: PALMS OF THE WORLD ONLINE
An authoritative online palm encyclopaedia
www.palmweb.org

PLANT ILLUSTRATIONS
A website wonderfully rich in copyright-free palm illustrations
www.plantillustrations.org

ROUNDTABLE ON SUSTAINABLE PALM OIL (RSPO)
With a membership including palm oil producers and processors,
consumer goods manufacturers and environmental NGOs, RSPO
promotes the production and use of sustainable palm oil
www.rspo.org

ROYAL BOTANIC GARDENS, KEW
The world's most famous botanic garden with an iconic palm house.
The wide-ranging website rewards deep burrowing
www.kew.org

Acknowledgements

Although it did not take quite as much time for this book to be written as it takes for either the Tahina palm (*Tahina spectabilis*) or the talipot palm (*Corypha umbraculifera*) to flower, this writing project has taken an inordinately long period to complete. I would like to express my gratitude to Michael Leaman of Reaktion Books for his extravagant patience and to thank his colleagues for turning my words into this book.

A host of friends and colleagues at the University of Sussex provided helpful palm insights and comments. They include Mike Boice, Persephone Deacon, the late Giles Dickins, Tony Fielding, River Jones, Laurence Koffman, the late Chris Marlin, Geoffrey Mead, Kate O'Riordan, Sara Parker, David Rudling, Martin Ryle and Paul Yates. Particular thanks are due to Alexandra Loske for sharing her palm knowledge, guiding me around the Brighton Royal Pavilion cast-iron palm trees and introducing me to the decorative use of palms in Germany, including the Zwiefalten Abbey confessionals and the Chinese Teahouse at Sanssouci Park in Potsdam.

Valuable material, ideas or perspectives were also provided by Julia Barfield and David Marks; Hope Ibeawuchi Beales and Roz Shipway; Allan Brodie; Hanna Büdenbender; Frank and Onra Coffey; Elizabeth Draper; Jim Heath; Tom Holland; Audrey and David Simpson; Kate Soper; Stephen Walker; David Ward and Gary Winter; Keith Barry of Christian Heritage London at St Botolph without Aldersgate; Saint Lucia's Kurt 'Island Man' Joseph; Christopher Mills of the Royal Botanic Gardens, Kew; Nicky Wharton of Trebah Garden, Cornwall; and Ben Wilson in Palm Cove, Cairns, Australia. Where I was uncertain about the botany, Hugh Pritchard of the Royal Botanic Gardens was generous in commentating on particular chapters. Particular thanks are due to Mary Hoar who read and commented on the manuscript.

Family members including Jamila Al Adwani and Ron Gray, Tristan French and Fredericka Gray, and Holly, Jack and Stephen Gray sometimes joined me as palm accomplices, while Carol Gray has been my constant fellow traveller to varied real and imaginary palm lands.

Photo Acknowledgements

ॐ

The author and publishers wish to express their thanks to the below sources of illustrative material and/or permission to reproduce it:

From Jean Barbot, *A Description of the Coasts of North and South-Guinea: and of the Ethiopia Inferior, Vulgarly Angola . . .* (London, 1732): p. 72; Basel Mission Archives (ref. no. QD-34.001.0019): p. 93; © Hope Ibeawuchi Beales: pp. 89, 109, 111; © Daniel Beltrá (courtesy of Catherine Edelman Gallery, Chicago): p. 124; Brooklyn Museum: p. 54 (bottom); © Rhett A. Butler, Mongabay: pp. 106–7, 118, 120; Centre for the Study of World Christianity, University of Edinburgh: p. 94; Craig, via Wikimedia Commons: p. 123; Dixson Galleries, State Library of New South Wales, Australia: p. 76; © Eden Project: p. 176; courtesy Getty Open Content Program: pp. 60, 61, 64; Fred Gray: pp. 8, 10, 11, 12, 19, 20, 26, 27, 28, 31, 33, 36, 55, 71, 102, 134, 135, 139, 145, 146, 147, 151, 152 (top and bottom), 154, 164, 167, 172, 173, 174, 184 (top and bottom), 186, 190, 192; Carol M. Highsmith collection/Library of Congress, Washington, DC: pp. 34–5, 137, 140; Kunsthalle, Hamburg: p. 163; © David Hockney/Collection Tate Gallery, London: p. 9; from Louis van Houtte, *Flore des serres et des jardins de l'Europe*, vol. V (Ghent, 1849): p. 6; from Hermann Adolph Köhler, *Köhler's Medizinal-Pflanzen in naturgetreuen Abbildungen mit kurz erläuterndem Texte: Atlas zur Pharmacopoea germanica etc . . .*, vol. III (Gera, 1887): pp. 74, 90; Library of Congress, Washington, DC: pp. 40 (top and bottom), 42, 54 (top), 81, 169; courtesy © Alexandra Loske: pp. 180, 181; from Carl Friedrich Philipp von Martius, *Historia naturalis palmarum*, vols I–II (Leipzig, 1823–50): p. 22; Metropolitan Museum of Art, New York: pp. 38, 45, 46, 47, 50, 52, 58, 62, 65, 92, 103, 130, 185, 178; from Sophy Moody, *The Palm Tree* (London, 1864): pp. 18, 85; from *Mr Punch on his Travels* (New Punch Library, c. 1930): p. 189; NASA: p. 119; NASA/GSFC/METI/ ERSDAC/JAROS and U.S./Japan ASTER Science Team: p. 187; New York Public Library Digital Collections: p. 17; Rijksmuseum, Amsterdam: pp. 66, 77; from Sylvia Leith-Ross, *African Conversation Piece* (1944): p. 96; The Royal Pavilion, Art Gallery and Museums, Brighton: p. 182; Science Museum/London Wellcome Images: pp. 15, 68; from Berthold Seemann, *Popular History of the Palms and Their Allies* (London, 1856): pp. 86, 158; courtesy Trebah Garden, Cornwall: p. 149; U.S. National Archives and Records Administration:

Index